Mr. H

the

Chorus Master

Dedicated to the memory
of my brother Roger.

the Mr. Hill Chorus Master

A musical journey through the lives of three 19th century Norwich musicians

by Pauline Stratton

Front Cover:
The list of Chorus Members from the 1842 Norfolk & Norwich Triennial festival
by kind permission of the Norfolk Record Office

ISBN: 0 900616 61 X

Printed and Published by
Geo. R. Reeve Ltd., 9-11 Town Green, Wymondham, Norfolk.

PREFACE

John Hill and two of his sons contributed greatly to the musical life of Norwich and Norfolk between 1824 and 1900. They received high praise for their talents, dedication and achievements which extended not only to the amateur choral and instrumental societies of the city but to many towns and villages throughout Norfolk including Diss, North Walsham, Dereham and Wymondham.

As I discovered the extent of their contribution to local music, a valuable part of Norfolk's past became unveiled which had remained hidden for over a century. I realised this was information which had to be shared. So, although no literary scholar, I have compiled this book reconstructing their lives through the musical, social and topical events of the period.

I felt John, James Frederick, Horace and their friends worthy of a place in history. I hope you do too.

Contents

PART 1

JOHN HILL.

PART II

JAMES FREDERICK HILL.

PART III

HORACE HILL.

Illustrations

* = see notes at end of chapter
( ) = see source of information at end of part.

PART I

JOHN HILL

CHAPTER 1.

The Norfolk and Norwich Musical Festival of 1824.

The Norfolk and Norwich hospital, a charitable institution, opened in 1772. Each year a special service was preached in the cathedral and a collection taken for the hospital. The service was later replaced by a performance of an oratorio in Assize week. The amount of money collected became but a trifle and the hospital governors felt they could no longer impose on the musical gentlemen concerned. In October 1823 a letter appeared in the local newspapers drawing attention to the hospital's severe financial state and their plan to raise money by holding a musical festival in 1824. Not willing to risk any of their own dwindling funds, the hospital invited friends of the institution to enter into a conditional subscription to indemnify the hospital against any loss incurred, stressing that the sums subscribed would only be required if the festival made a loss but they had every confidence it would be a success.

A promise of at least £500 was required, within a short space of time guarantees amounted to £2500. This overwhelming response not only secured any risk but also illustrated the great interest in supporting such a venture.

A festival committee was formed and plans were put in motion to make the Norfolk and Norwich festival as magnificent as England's other major musical festivals.

George Smart was approached to be the conductor. Permission was obtained from the corporation for the use of St. Andrew's Hall and also for the erection of an organ at the west end. The dates of 21st to 24th September 1824 were secured to give 3 evening miscellaneous concerts, 3 morning oratorios and a Grand Ball to conclude on the evening of 24th.

King George IV became patron. The Dukes of Gloucester, York and Sussex, vice patrons. The Hon. J. Wodehouse accepted the presidency and many local people of "quality" acquired the title of Vice President.

The musical arrangements were entrusted to R. Bacon*, E. Taylor* and J. Athow and by their instigation Gray of London was instructed to erect the organ. The firm allowed the committee the

9

St. Andrew's Hall Interior

option of hire or purchase of the instrument, so the organ was hired for the duration of the festival for the sum of £94-10s-0d (1). The Rev Elwin* was appointed organist. A choral society of some 105 local voices was formed under the direction of E. Taylor and rehearsals started in December 1823.

Well known soloist were engaged including Miss Stephens and Miss Salmon for £190 each, Miss Carew for £70, Sgn & Mme de Begnis for £210 and Mr. Vaughan* for £84. (2)

By early September work inside the hall was complete. The patrons gallery, side galleries and orchestra had been constructed. The seats, with back rests for extra comfort, covered in crimson cloth. At the east end between the columns, the tiered seating of the patrons gallery reached to the top of Nelson's portrait. These seats were available to anyone wishing to purchase a 1 guinea ticket. The first stage of the gallery was left free, enabling it to be furnished with more comfortable chairs for the most distinguished of guests. Side galleries occupied the full width of the aisles; the seats rising to a height above all the portraits excepting that of Alderman Hawkes on the north side.

The floor was covered with deal planks to aid the comfort of those who choose to sit thereon and to provide a better dancing surface for the ball. The organ, erected above the orchestra, was "a grand and powerful instrument" being, except for the addition of a clarion, the same composition as the great organ in the cathedral, with a compass of FFF to F in alt.

Rumours spread of smallpox in the city. On 10th September a statement was printed in the press from the superintendents of the city's poor announcing the city had no cases of the disease in the last 6 months. However, as a precautionary measure, the gentlemen of the vaccination committee recommended that the poorer classes should be vaccinated.

On the evening of the 11th September St. Andrew's Hall was opened to the public. For the admission charge of 1/-, 703 respectable persons of both sexes came to view the new gas illuminations and to listen to the organ. Gas burners fixed to radiations of brasswork poured forth their flames from beneath the capitals of the columns and above the orchestra. The light they created was said to be more vivid than that of day. The organ was still incomplete as Mr. E. Pettet, Mr. James Taylor, Mr. Woolman and Mr. Westropp entertained those assembled by playing voluntaries. Mr. Buck, the cathedral organist, was unable to offer his services that evening; he was suffering from an inflammatory disorder of the eyes. However his recovery was sufficient enough, by the following Wednesday to perform alongside Mr. Pettet, to a further 700 visitors.

The organ was completed by the following Saturday; the clarion and trumpet stops having been added. George Smart, who had been in the city since Tuesday, conducted rehearsals and also assisted in the playing of the organ as a further 2000 visitors viewed the hall.

Tickets for the festival could be purchased from 13th September at Mr. Page's room opposite St. Andrew's Hall between 10am and 4pm. During the festival week this was extended to 9am until

10pm. The city's bankers supplied a clerk each day. Every evening the accounts were made up and the money paid into Tompson, Barclay and Ives bank (2) in Orford Hill.(3)

There was scepticism that the festival would fail owing to other attractions in the city. Finch's Ranelagh Gardens was open for the whole week and the theatre was staging Shakespeare's "Othello" as well as the pantomime, "Whittington and his Cat".

Festival ticket sales on the first day amounted to £126-10s-0d. On Monday 20th, the day before the festival, these had risen to £337-4s-0d. This day was one of continuous rain preventing some of the performers attending the final rehearsals. One of the soloists, Mr. Sapio, had arrived too ill to perform, so Mr. Cummins, a violinist, was hastily sent to London to engage the services of Garcia (2).

The city's choral society had been augmented by singers from New College Oxford, King's and Trinity College Cambridge, Ely Cathedral, Windsor Chapel, and principal chorus singers from London, making a total of 35 trebles, 30 countertenors, 35 tenors and 40 basses. One of the tenors was Mr. Hill.

The orchestra included 20 first violins, 20 second violins, 16 violas, 9 cellos, 8 double basses plus tromboni and serpent players from His Majesty's Household Band. Mr. F. Cramer and Kiesewetter were appointed leaders of the orchestra.

On Tuesday afternoon despite more rain, county families flocked into the city, some staying for the duration of the festival. A list of suitable lodgings could be obtained from the Secretary to the Norfolk and Norwich Hospital, Mr Deacon, in St. Andrew's Broad Street. The newspapers also carried private advertisements. Close to the hall a property boasting a large dining room, 2 chambers, with use of kitchen, linen and servants was available on application to Mr. Powley of Elm Hill.

As darkness fell, the roads leading to St. Andrew's Hall became crowded with people. Passageways were kept clear for carriages and those on foot to the 4 entrances (Great South door, Elm Hill, St. George's Bridge St. and the Garden door) by a mounted detachment of the 2nd Dragoon Guards.

Many complimentary tickets had been allotted to persons including Mrs. Sophia Buck, Mrs Pettet and Mr. Stannard who had freely ornamented the front of the orchestra. Some 50 gratuitous performers also received a free ticket to admit one person into any concert (2).

At 7 o'clock the doors of the hall opened. Entry was by ticket only. No money was allowed to change hands on the door. The 1 guinea patrons gallery tickets were 'check', to distinguish them from the half guinea tickets for the side galleries and floor. Some 900 people had taken their places when the cheering outside hailed the arrival of the Duke of Sussex. On his entry to the hall by the Great South door the audience rose to their feet, clapping as he was conducted to his seat in the patrons gallery by the mayor, Mr. H. Francis. The Duke then bowed to them in recognition of his welcome.

The programme commenced with Haydn's Sinfonia No 8, after which the National Anthem was sung. George Smart then came forward to announce that, due to a "domestic calamity" Mr. F. Novello was unable to fulfil his solo role so Mr. E. Taylor very kindly agreed to take his place. The concert proceeded with a glee by Horsley "By Celia's Arbour All the Night" sung by Messrs. Terrail, Vaughan, Taylor and Bellamy. Several vocal works by Rossini and an unspecified violoncello concerto played by Lindley were also included in the programme. Lindley's concerto unfortunately did little to delight the audience.

The second act began with the overture from Cherubini's "Anacreon" and ended with a Terzetto, "Ricciardo e Zoraide" by Rossini.

After the concert those who had come by carriage remained inside the hall until a festival official announced the arrival of their transport. Carriages leaving by the Great South door proceeded along St. Andrew's St.; those leaving from the Elm Hill entrance departed via St. Simon's church and Tombland.

Wednesday morning's grand concert of sacred music, in 3 parts, opened with the first verse of Handel's "Dettingen Te Deum", "We Praise Thee O God". Other airs and choruses by this great master featured prominently in the programme with the addition of items such as "Gratias Agimus" by Guglielmi* sung by Miss Salmon. The audience obeyed their instructions not to clap during the performance of sacred music and the concert concluded with the chorus "Hosanna to the Son of David" by O. Gibbons with an instrumental accompaniment arranged especially for the occasion by E. Taylor. The Duke was impressed with the concert remarking that no where had he "heard choruses so good".

Wednesday evening's miscellaneous concert, was attended by the Earl of Albemarle accompanied by the countess. Mozart's

Sinfonia in E♭ commenced the programme. Mr. Bellamy sang the air "Battle of Hohenlinden" by C. Smith. Although he was obviously suffering from an indisposition, he coped most successfully. The quintett "Blow Gently Gales" from Bishop's "The Slave", having been perfectly sung by Miss Stephens, Miss Carew and Messrs Terrail, Vaughan and Bellamy received an encore.

Garcia was warmly greeted with great applause. His rich toned voice possessed an extensive compass making him a gentleman with a high reputation.

The only oratorio performed in its entirety was the "Messiah" on Thursday morning. People arrived early. By eleven o'clock every space on the floor was taken and the side galleries were well occupied. The Duke arrived at half past eleven accompanied by his host the Bishop of Norwich. They took their places in the patrons gallery alongside Lord Albemarle, Col. Wodehouse, the Mayor, the High Sheriff and the Dean.

One of 4 choir boys from King's, Master Kempton, sang the solo "He Shall Feed His Flock". Some 75 years later Kempton recalled the occasion, (5) describing how he had travelled by post chaise, and at Scole, picked up the stage coach to Norwich. In St. Andrew's Hall he had sat behind the ladies in the front row and was helped down by Miss Stephens to sing his solo. Miss Carew then asked him to stay and sing with her. Kempton was just 12 years and 10 months old but could remember how proud he had felt. After so many years he could still recall how Lindley broke a string on his violoncello as he accompanied a lady soloist, causing him to apologise profoundly for "spoiling her solo". Mr. Harper's playing of the trumpet obligato to Bellamy's rendition of "The Trumpet Shall Sound" sent a thrill of excitement through the whole audience and the word "Hallelujah" was not uniformly pronounced by the chorus; the result being quite noticeable.

That evening the boys were treated to a fireworks display in Ranelagh Gardens.

Kempton's recollections regarding the trumpet obligato were endorsed by the press who referred to it as "astonishing", but Master Kempton's singing was thought to have been rather timid.

On Thursday evening St. Andrew's Hall was filled to capacity by half past seven with 2066 visitors. Over 300 more were turned away at the door. This popular concert commenced with

Beethoven's C minor symphony but the music was lost in the gradual tranquillisation of the vast audience. In the middle of the first 'act' the Duke rose from his seat requesting that gentlemen offered their seats to the many ladies who were standing. He then seated himself on the gallery floor.

Two airs by Bishop, "Should he upbraid" and the Echo Song "What airy sound", both sung by Miss Stephens, were encored. J. S. Smith's glee "Blest pair of Sirens", a cantata "Alexis" by Pepusch; a fantasia for clarinet by Baermann and a violin concert by Mayseder also featured in the programme. The solo part of the latter being exquisitely played by Kiesewetter.

The concert concluded with Mozart's overture to "Die Zauberflöte".

Friday morning's programme comprised of 3 acts. The first being a selection of pieces by Mozart and Handel with the exception of "Te Ergo" (Te Deum) by Graun. The second, passages from Haydn's "Creation" with the choral burst on the word "LIGHT" being so forcefully rendered it overpowered some of the listeners. The third act featured double concertos by Handel. Between an air from "Solomon" and another from "Saul" was Mr. Perry's* chorus "Give the Lord" from his oratorio "The Death of Abel". His work was thought to have been placed in a very perilous yet honourable position. It was judged worthy of its place.

The musical part of the festival closed with "Sing Ye The Lord" from Handel's "Israel in Egypt".

The Friday evening ball, with an entrance cost of 15/- including refreshments, attracted 1152 ladies and gentlemen. A further 283 paid 5/- to sit in the vacant section of the orchestra to watch the spectacle. The hall floor was so crowded that the dance band, led by Mr. Leitolff, could hardly be heard, the quadrilles therefore gave little enjoyment. The Duke retired at 2 o'clock in the morning and it was half past two before the crowd had thinned sufficiently to allow any fashionable dances to be entered into with spirit.

The festival had been a tremendous success, with receipts totalling £6695-3s-6d. Donations of £545-2s-0d had also been received including £105 from the corporation and £50 from the Archbishop of Canterbury. 6782 visitors had paid to view the preparations of the hall.

For their part in the festival Garcia received £157-10s-0d., the 4 boys from King's a total of £20 (2) and Mr. Hill £2-2s-0d (2).

In addition to his fee of £105, George Smart was presented with a gold snuff box costing £36-9s-0d (2) and also granted the freedom of the city and county. (4)

A silver waiter costing £52-10s-0d was presented to Edward Taylor (2) for raising and training of the Choral Society and the Rev. Elwin was offered a piece of plate which he declined.

After the payment of expenses, £2411-4s-2d was given to the hospital. (4)

In October the corporation agreed to purchase the Gray organ for 280 guineas (4) and at a meeting of the hospital governors, Taylor expressed the view that if the musical standard of the chorus was to be preserved for future festivals, the number of singers would need to be increased and a room, such as the concert room near to St. George's Bridge, hired for practice. (6)

In 1825 Edward Taylor left Norfolk for a new career in London. To mark his departure he was presented with a richly chased silver coffee pot, cream ewer and sugar basin on an elegant silver stand inscribed "Presented to Edward Taylor by his friends and fellow citizens on his removal from Norwich. In testimony of their esteem for his character and of their regret of his departure".

* *Bacon, Richard Mackenzie. Proprietor of the Norwich Mercury. He also assisted with the production of the "Quarterly Musical Magazine and Review," the first journal in England to be devoted to music. (12)*

* *Elwin, Robert Fountaine. Rector of St. Margaret's church, Norwich. His paternal grandfather married the grand daughter of Oliver Cromwell. Elwin died in Leeds 21st February 1853.*

Guglielmi. 1727-1804. Composer/performer of operas, oratorios and chamber music, who visited London in 1768. In 1793 Guglielmi retired from the stage and accepted the post of Maestro at the Vatican. The air "Gratias Agimus" was very popular in England. (12)

*Perry, George Frederick. Born in Norwich in 1793. Became a cathedral chorister under Dr. Beckwith. After leaving the cathedral he studied the violin and was leader of the theatre's band. In 1822 he moved to London taking up a similar post at the Haymarket Theatre. Perry had an incredible musical memory, comparable to that of Mozart. His oratorio "The Death of Abel" was composed whilst living in Norwich. (12)

*Taylor, Edward. Born in Norwich in 1784. Taylor received his musical education from Beckwith but was an ironmonger by trade. He was sheriff of Norwich in 1819. After an unsuccessful attempt at civil engineering in London, Taylor followed a career in music and in 1837 was appointed professor of music at Gresham College. (12)

* Vaughan, Thomas. Born in Norwich in 1782 and a chorister under Dr Beckwith. In 1799 he became a lay-clerk at St. George's Chapel, Windsor and 4 years later, a gentleman of the Chapel Royal. At about the same time he was appointed vicar-choral of St. Paul's Cathedral and lay-vicar of Westminster Abbey. Vaughan died in 1843 and was buried in the cloisters of Westminster Abbey. (12)

CHAPTER 2

John Hill Appointed Chorus Master.

Following Taylor's departure, the Norwich Choral Society amalgamated with the Ladies Choral Society to form The Choral Society under the direction of the Rev. R. F. Elwin with John Hill as chorus master. John was 27 years old and had received his singing tuition from Taylor.

During 1825, it came to the attention of R. Bacon that King George IV had a number of copies of Dr. Arnold's edition of Handel's works. The King was willing to bestow the scores, on request, to choral societies who held festivals. The Norfolk and Norwich festival committee made an enquiry and in the summer of 1825, 49 volumes were dispatched by Mack & Sons, Waggoners, of Cripplegate to Mr. Deacon of the hospital. (6)

On examination of the concert room, a perfectly dry place was found in a room under the orchestra to store the scores. A deal closet 5 feet long, 18 inches high and 14 inches deep with folding doors was made and affixed to the wall. Each volume was stamped "Presented to the Norfolk and Norwich Hospital by King George IV". (6)

Choral concerts were performed during 1826, the receipts from which supported the Society. One such concert took place on May 26th in the Hall Concert Room. It was limited to an audience of 200, paying an entrance charge of 5/-. The chorus was assisted by soloists Miss Cramer, Miss Wensley and Mr. Penson. Glees, choruses from Bishop's "Law of Java" and "Guy Mannering" and the overture to the "Barber of Seville" were performed. "The chorusses went off with a precision that reflected credit upon those which took part". The event was poorly attended and the public were criticised for their lack of support. It was pointed out that such concerts were vital if a high standard was to be maintained for the next festival.

At the time improvements were being made to a "concert room organ". On 4th February 1826 a payment of £2-4s-0d was made to Mr. Steel for "7 large organ pipes" for this instrument (2) and in May, a stool costing 12/- was made for the organist. (2)

John Hill was the chorus master for the 1827 festival. Edward Taylor returned to the city to sing in the chorus. The festival followed the same form as in 1824. Alterations had been made to the hall organ, £1-5s-6d being paid for "long movements.....mandrils and drawstop heads". The resident singers with John Hill and the instrumentalists under the leadership of Cotton Reeve, the 2nd violinist of the festival band, practised nearly every evening.

The first general rehearsal of the 219 instrumentalists, 50 trebles, 45 altos, 55 tenors and 60 basses did not take place until the 17th September. It was the day before the first concert and rehearsals continued from 10am until 6pm.

The following evening the streets filled with people making their way to St. Andrew's Hall. Carriages stretched from the Great South door of the hall to the Market Place and from the Elm Hill entrance to Tombland; their passage through the crowded streets being cleared by the 12th Royal Lancers. Notices had been pinned to all of the entrances explaining that the violinist, Kiesewetter, was too ill to perform and his place as leader of the band was to be taken by Mr. Cramer (6). Kiesewetter had arrived in Norwich in deplorable health, not wanting to miss his engagement. Although too weak to perform he still received his fee. This programme of miscellaneous works included the glee "Go Idle Boy" by Dr. Callcott which had won an award some 20 years earlier at the Catch Club. It was sung by Terrail, Whall, Vaughan and Taylor. Miss Bacon made her first appearance before an audience in her native city, singing "Serena i vaghi rai" from Rossini's "Semiramide"

After the concert, several gentlemen had their pockets picked as they left the hall. The Bow Street Runners, employed to assist the police, recognised 3 known criminals who made off through the crowds. 6 suspect characters were committed to the Bridewell for further examination.

On Wednesday morning the audience heard Perry's anthem "Lord of all Power" from his oratorio "The Fall of Jerusalem" sung from the manuscript. Perry presided at the organ. He was thought at the time, to be a composer of great merit. Haydn's Mass No 2 was also performed; it having been adapted to English words especially for the festival by Edward Taylor.

In the evening a loud crash panicked the audience. On investigation it was found to have been caused by violin cases falling on the long movement of the organ. The heavy rain leaked through a hole in the hall roof, dripping into the piano which spoiled the player's accompaniment to the vocal items.

The hall was filled on Thursday morning with people eager to hear Handel's "Messiah". Miss Stephens, who had so far been indisposed, sang for the first time. Her voice struggling "hard against the rising anguish in her filial bosom pierced with great sorrow for her father's recent death".

Kiesewetter was still too ill to take part in Thursday evening's concert. Instead Master Blagrove, a twelve year old student of the RAM, played the first movement of a violin concerto by Rode in a "masterly style".

Friday morning found the hall again full to overflowing. This time a selection of pieces from Handel's oratorios and motets by Mozart formed the programme.

The festival's total attendance exceeded that of 1824 by 326. After the payment of expenses which include £15-15s-0d to Master Blagrove, £12 to Gray for attendance on the organ, with an additional payment of £57-10s-0d on 27th September for materials and complete repair of the instrument; £1-12s-0d for coach hire for the ladies of the choral society and £12-0s-6d for beer, a profit of £1672-12s-1d was given to the hospital. (7)

One of the festival's programme sellers, James Bailey, had been forcefully carried away on the 10th September by the Blue and Whites to prevent him voting in the Alderman election on the 12th. He was first held at the Wroxham Castle public house, then moved to the Swan at Horning; onto Smallburgh and then to the Plough at Ridlington before being returned to the city in a poor state of health. Despite his condition he still carried out his duties during the festival. He died on 22nd September from a "broken blood vessel". A jury decided he had "Died from a visitation of God" (4).

CHAPTER 3

Pedal Pipes

On 28th February 1828 John Hill received £10 for "drilling the choir" (2). Norwich was experiencing difficult times. Weavers were rioting and thieves were executed on Castle Hill watched by crowds of spectators, many of whom were women with children (4). By the 1830 musical festival John was living in Ber Street and was a tailor by trade (8). He assisted George Smart with the rehearsals "giving his time". In the chorus was Kempton from Canterbury, a countertenor and among the choir boys from the cathedral was a Master Hill (9).

In the Wednesday morning concert another extract from Perry's "Fall of Jerusalem" was heard; "Blow ye Trumpets". Perry conducted. Smart presided at the organ. Heavy rain again caused problems throughout the festival and Lindley was forced to perform his violin concerto under an umbrella.

In 1833 the county was experiencing a depression. Cholera was in parts of the country. Agriculture and trade were poor. The recent elections had caused rioting in the streets of Norwich with the polling booth for the "orange and purple" being burnt down and the 7th Hussars called to restore order (4). Friction was also growing between Elwin and Smart. Elwin had never agreed with Smart receiving the freedom of the city.

In January 1833 it was felt the festival should be postponed until 1834, but at a meeting in May this sentiment was reversed by those who thought a music festival would raise the public's morale. As only £1600 could be mustered in guarantees, the vocalists and instrumentalists agreed to accept a reduced fee.

During 1832 the organ had been cleaned and repaired by Abel for £1-0s-0d and tuned on at least 3 occasions. A Mr. Freeman received £2-6s-0d for gilding the organ pipes. (9)

At the opening concert on 17th September 1833 the National Anthem was played from memory, the orchestral parts having mistakenly not been handed out. Taylor sang his composition "Away away on the sparkling tide" which was warmly received, being described as "an excellent composition sung powerfully and well". The musical treat of the evening however was the violinist, De Beriot, playing a concerto of his own composition. It was his first appearance in the city.

On the Wednesday morning Spohr's "Last Judgement" was heard in its entirety for the first time in England, only extracts having been previously performed.

Friday's oratorio, "The Deluge" (Die Sündfluth) by Schneider, translated from the German to English by Taylor, received its first performance in England. Some felt it an unwise choice for the festival, preferring instead Handel's "Messiah". "The Deluge" was criticised for being "devoid of originality" for it was evident that Scheidner had studied the works of Haydn.

After the festival John Hill received a payment of £20 for 3 years attendance as chorus master (9). 13 of Mr. Hill's pupils, one of whom was a Master Harcourt, were paid a total of £5-18s-0d (9) and John Hill's glee singers received £4 for entertaining at the open evenings in the hall prior to the festival. Elwin received £11-1s-9d for repairing the St. Andrew's Hall organ, fixing the long movement, tuning the instrument and for his attendance both at rehearsals and throughout the festival.

Unlike previous occasions, all the profit from the festival, was not given to the Norfolk and Norwich Hospital. Instead it was shared between the hospital, receiving £336-2s-9d, the Norwich Dispensary, £37-7s-0d; the Eye Infirmary, £37-7s-0d; and the Institute for the Indigent Blind, £37-6s-11d.

The choral society continued to hold concerts during 1834 and 1835. One such occasion took place in St. Andrew's Hall on a Tuesday evening in February 1834, when works by Handel, Haydn and Mozart were heard. The performers included Bexfield, Harcourt, and Hill with Mr. Hill doing "himself great credit in his recitatives, he sang them like a musician".

At about that time an organ for the Bridge St. concert room was purchased for £63-0s-0d. In April 1835 Fox provided pine for pedal pipes for this instrument at a cost of £25-12s-0d. Abel and his assistants repaired the soundboard, movement and bellows for £8-0s-0d and a half yearly rent of £2-10s-0d was paid for an organ warehouse (9).

During 1835 the ceiling in St. Andrew's Hall was repaired by the corporation, turning the hall from one of the worst to one of the best concert halls for sound. Work was also carried out on the Gray organ as £5-8s-6d was paid for "cutting St. Andrew's Hall organ to pitch". Elwin was in charge of adding pedal pipes to this instrument, paying Abel and his assistants £36-7s-0d for fixing the new pedal pipes and Fox £25-12s-0d for the pine. Sundry expenses for nails, glue, paint, deal, wainscot, mahogany, skins and candles amounted to £5-17s-0d. 4 bellows blowers earned a total of £1-13s-0d when the pipes were tuned (9).

The pedal division was completed in readiness for the 1836 festival. A double row of pedal pipes flanked either side of the original organ; the wind being supplied by separate bellows and windchest. The largest pipe FFFF was 24 feet in length, 27 inches wide outside and 24 inches wide inside. Various coats of arms edged by gothic panels emblazoned the surface. Elwin had spent £317 creating an organ of "stupendous size" which filled the entire 32 feet space between the pillars. Stannard the carpenter was paid £67-0-6d for making "a frame and enclosure for the pipes", Mr. Russell fixed the long movement to the pedal pipes and Mr. Watts made weights and a cast iron plate for the bellows (9).

Turle of Westminster Abbey was engaged as the festival organist receiving £31-10s-0d, assisted by Mr. E. Clare of Norwich who received £6-6s-0d (9). Organists from St. Paul's Cathedral, the Chapel Royal, Southwell, Grantham and Oldham came to hear the instrument.

More than 200 of the 270 strong chorus for the 1836 festival were weavers, dyers, tailors and shoemakers of Norwich. A Miss Hill sang in the trebles for a payment of £1-5s-0d and Master Hill received 5/-. J.W. Hill in the altos was paid £1-10s-0d. A pale thin youth, Mr. Blagrove, led the orchestra (9).

Edward Taylor's controversial piece "Redemption" was performed on the Wednesday morning. He had turned Mozart's Requiem into an oratorio by adding airs and recitatives. Mozart's andante from the overture to "Don Giovanni", an air from "Tito", and a Bach chorale were woven into the score. He had also compiled a completely new text in English. Critics cried out that Taylor should never have tampered with this divine work, coming from Mozart's departing spirit. It had been written with the intention of being part of a catholic service, not for entertainment.

The Requiem had never been heard in England for most festivals took place in Anglican churches thus prohibiting a work of this nature. Taylor's "Redemption" was therefore a way of bringing the Requiem to an English audience.

Bishop's cantata "The Seventh Day" was performed on Thursday morning. It was preceded by Haydn's "Creation", both composers using texts by Milton. Bishop's work had been composed for the London Philharmonic season of 1834 on the understanding it would not appear on any other programme for at least 2 years; that time had just elapsed.

The new organ pedals demonstrated their effectiveness in the anthem "Have Mercy Lord". This work was termed as Beethoven's funeral anthem but was Elwin adaptation of the 90th psalm set to one of Beethoven's "Equali" which had been performed at the composer's funeral.

At the close of Friday's concert Elwin made a speech praising Taylor and Hill. Smart, despite having "worked like Hercules" was not mentioned.

The festival made a loss of £231-5s-10d (9) and the rift between Elwin and Smart deepened as each blamed the other for the short fall. To help to restore a monetary balance Hudson Gurney donated £50, Smart £15, no beer was to be provided at future rehearsals and the concert room organ was sold for £120 to the Old Meeting House in Colegate.

An advertisement was placed in the newspaper for the sale of the instrument. Two organs were advertised as "For Sale" around that time. Firstly, on February 25th 1837, "A fine toned organ suitable for church or chapel in an oak case with speaking front containing 8 stops in the great and 3 in the swell with an octave of pedals. For price and particulars apply to Rev. Elwin, King St." Then on 16th December 1837 the following advertisement appeared; "An organ suited to a church or large chapel with 2 rows of keys and pedals. There are 9 stops in the great organ and 3 in the swell and a double diapason in the pedal with coupler movement. The case is of ancient carved oak and is 13ft high, 8ft wide and 6ft deep....... For price and particulars apply to the Rev. Elwin or the keeper of St Andrew's Hall who will show the instrument".

On 26th May 1837 Messrs. Hill and Buck were chorus master and organist at a special performance of the "Messiah" for the benefit of the widow of Alfred Pettet (organist of St Peter Mancroft). The admittance charge was 5/- or 5 tickets could be bought for 1 guinea. The concert surpassed all expectations both in attendance and effectiveness of performance with choir boys, Furze and Brown, from the cathedral, singing their airs delightfully. None of the 250 performers requested payment and no complimentary tickets were handed out. A sum of £150 was presented to Mrs Pettet. Buck collected a similar amount in donations with which an annuity was purchased for the widow.

At a meeting of the hospital committee in October 1837, the Rev. Fellowes expressed concern over the festival. He felt instead of raising funds for the hospital it was causing funds to deplete, for people no longer bequeathed sums of money to them.

The choral society was thus reformed under new management. The £100 per year it received from the hospital ceased and instead the society raised funds by annual subscription. The concerts continued with John Hill as chorus master and Buck as organist. More than 800 attended their first concert, a performance of "Israel in Egypt", under the new management.

The question of whether the festival should carry on without the support of the hospital caused much debate but it was decided to press ahead after a motion in favour of continuing was won by just one vote.

CHAPTER 4

Spohr's Year

A newly formed madrigal society under the conductorship of John Hill held their first meeting in the library room of St. Andrew's Hall in January 1838. Some 40 members gathered together to sing works by Wilbye, Weelkes, Gibbons, and a recent addition to the repertoire by John's son James Frederick, "I saw fair Chloris walk alone". James Frederick was a pupil of Buck and his madrigal had been recognised by the London Madrigal Society into whose stock it had been received. The melody was elegant and the harmonies reminiscent of those of Byrd and Gibbons "not a single modern phrase" could be detected. Those present exclaimed they had "seldom passed an evening of such unmixed enjoyment" and it was hoped the society would hire a larger room in the future so their meetings could be opened to the public at a moderate charge.

The choral society's concerts continued with increased success. Their spring concert in April 1838, a performance of the "Creation", drew an attendance of 1350 including all the "rank and fashion" of the city and county.

The festival in 1839 became known as Spohr's year on account of the composer coming to conduct the first performance of his oratorio "Calvary". Spohr had not been to England for 20 years and special parties were allowed each day to meet him. The festival conductor was Edward Taylor who had agreed to take on the task after Smart refused the position. Turle was the festival organist. Elwin had been busy altering the instrument and had made the keys "like an Irish gun - shoot round a corner" having "exactly reversed the usual position and the organist actually turned his back on the instrument". Spohr, accompanied by the mayor, attended Sunday morning service at the cathedral. The Rev. Storr of Otley, Suffolk preached the sermon. Some clergy were opposed to the intimacy of Spohr's libretto, believing it sinful and profane to use the suffering and death of Christ as a theme for music. Storr was one who felt this way. He implored his congregation, in which were present not only Spohr but the Bishop and many members of the festival committee, not to surrender their souls to one day of pleasure for those who attended the performance would be eternally damned. Luckily Spohr did not understand English. Each time he heard the name of his oratorio he smiled contentedly assuming it was being praised.

Storr's sermon had no effect. St. Andrew's Hall was full on Thursday morning to hear the work. An unusual deep calm fell over the hall just prior to the commencement of what was to be a superb performance. The work however proved unpopular in England. The Sacred Harmonic Society even dropped it from their Spohr festival of 1847.

Taylor's lack of ability as a conductor was severely criticised, several obvious mishaps having occurred during the festival. Many felt Smart should have conducted.

The festival made a profit of £1,295. £800 was given to charities and the remainder held over in a reserve fund. John Hill received his salary of £20, James Frederick received £10-0s-0d for copying "Calvary" and a further £7-10s-0d for playing the piano and organ (9).

In 1840 the festival committee purchased the scores and musical instruments belonging to the Norfolk and Norwich Hospital for £235.

John Hill's madrigal society gave their first public concert during February, in the Assembly House, performing secular and sacred madrigals from the 16th and 17th century, contrasting the rustic jollity of Weelkes to the solemnity of Tallis, the sacred works occupying the middle section of this 3 part programme. The room was agreeably full with respected company. It was evident from the singing that improvements had been made during the past year. The trebles sang in excellent tune with great sweetness in their voices and the whole performance was one of great precision.

Liszt's performance in the very same room a few months later however was not so well received; "our expectations of Liszt had been raised to the highest pitch may we confess we have been grievously disappointed. We listened in vain for one strain of pure and sustained melody or for one striking original harmony...His countenance, his conversation, his manner, and the eccentricity of his costume all conspired to proclaim him a man of no ordinary mind".

The 1841 choral concert series opened with a selection from Handel's "Jephtha". Mr. Yarington, a pupil of "our respected chorus master Mr. Hill", delivered the opening song steadily and effectively. Over 1000 persons had braved the January weather to sit in St Andrew's Hall which was for the first time warmed with gas stoves.

It was 16 years since John Hill was elected as chorus master of the choral society. He now lived in Cow Hill with his wife Sarah, daughter Elizabeth and sons Emanual, Henry, Horace and baby Alfred. (10)

On 10th December a charity concert was given in aid of the District Visiting Society and the Sick Poor Society. The admission: 3/-. John Hill was the chorus master, the organists Mr. Harcourt and James Frederick Hill. All the performers offered their services freely. Many, being weavers, were themselves suffering from severe destitution. The admirable discipline and "high conditions" of the chorus was attributed to the frequent and judicious training of John Hill. "The merit of this unassuming and excellent man's zeal and ability"..."deserves to be better known"..."not only in the musical world but to all who take an interest in the welfare of the various charitable institutions which have so largely benefited by his exertion".

Just a week prior to the concert John had journeyed to London to attend the first rehearsal of Spohr's new oratorio, "Fall of Babylon", at the Hanover Square room, his expenses of £5 (11) being reimbursed by the festival committee. The oratorio was to be the main attraction at the 1842 festival and had been written especially for the occasion on the suggestion of Taylor. The Hanover Square rehearsal enabled John to return to Norwich with a competent knowledge of the standard required by the Norwich Choral Society.

It was hoped Spohr would be able to conduct his work but despite a petition from Norwich, leave from his duties as conductor at the court opera of Cassel, was refused. The task was therefore entrusted to Taylor.

At the first evening concert of the festival, the excellent standard of the chorus was immediately evident from the singing of "God save the Queen"; their training being not of the popular "rail road" method, showed credit to their able and indefatigable Mr. Hill.

From 9 am on Thursday morning, carriages began to arrive in the city from all directions. Shortly after the hall doors opened the vast space inside was filled to excess.

Over 500 people had to be turned away. Taylor addressed the audience who were crammed into every corner, expressing his regret that the hall was not large enough. Those who found it too uncomfortable were given the opportunity to withdraw and attend instead one of the remaining concerts. Few left. The performance of the "Fall of Babylon" went extremely well, with great praise being bestowed upon the chorus for their precision "every light and shade, reflecting the highest credit" upon Mr Hill's method of training.

The festival gave £550 to charity from a profit of £716. Payments were made to Abel of £6-19s-0d for patching the pedal pipes and Theobald received 11/4d for supplying white skins for the organ. A new entrance had been made for the performers at a cost of £281-6s-1d by partitioning a passageway to the orchestra (11).

Throughout 1843 the choral concerts continued. Mr Braham's appearance in March attracted a large audience. This veteran tenor was reputed to be one of the finest of his time. He had sung publicly from the age of 10 and spent many years abroad where he performed at La Scala. All the concert tickets had been sold by mid afternoon. Towards the evening rain fell incessantly. Everyone who was able journeyed to St. Andrew's Hall by carriage. The Bridge St. entrance was opened early allowing 200 people to shelter from the weather until the doors opened. By 7.30pm every available seat in the hall was taken. More were brought and put wherever possible yet still people had to stand. Braham made his entrance after the opening overture, from Handel's "Esther". He received three rounds of hearty applause before singing pieces from "Jephtha". The chorus, "admirably trained by John Hill was in great strength". 1700 people had attended the concert, which raised £326-8s-0d.

John Hill's reputation as a tutor was growing. His singing classes were becoming very popular. In April, due to public demand he engaged an assistant, William Green, with the intention of holding classes on Saturday evenings at 8 o' clock in the Old Library Room of St. Andrew's Hall. This was in addition to the class held on Wednesday mornings at 11 o'clock. John also advertised that he was willing to undertake singing classes in any town or village within a 16 mile radius of Norwich. Applications could be made to Mr. Howlett of London St. or to John Hill at his residence at the corner of Cow Hill and St. Giles St.

The July choral society concert of 1843 was attended by the high sheriff and many of the "first" families of the city and county. Gratten Cooke played an oboe fantasia of his own composition. The work was based on an Indian air which had been sent to him

LIST OF PERFORMERS.

MADAME CARADORI ALLAN	MR. HOBBS
MISS RAINFORTH	MR. PHILLIPS
MISS MARIA B. HAWES	MR. BALFE
MISS BASSANO	MR. BRADBURY
	MR. YOUNG
AND	MR. WALTON
SIGNORA PACINI	AND
	SIGNOR RUBINI.

CONDUCTOR—PROFESSOR TAYLOR.

CHORUS.

FIRST TREBLES.		SECOND TREBLES.		SECOND TREBLES.	
Mrs Armes	Norwich	Master Beaney	Norwich	Pigg, A	Norwich
Miss Barchard	—	Beetley	..	Pigg, W	..
Blazer	..	Boltz	..	Pummell, W	..
Buttifant	..	Butcher, W	..	Pummell, T	..
Campling	..	Butcher, A	..	Skill, W	..
Mrs Cook	Ipswich	Church	..	Skill, T	..
Miss Cooke	Norwich	Cross	..	Skill, E	..
Dunn	London	Creed	..	Slipper	..
Dunn L	..	Cutting	..	Smith	..
Dunn, A	Norwich	Day, R	..	Thorne	..
Dye, K	..	Day, E	..	Wilkinson	..
Dye, E	..	Dunn	..	Williamson	..
Fuller	..	Esam	..		
Goffin	Yarmouth	Furze	..	FIRST ALTOS.	
Mrs Harcourt	Norwich	Gedge	..	Mr Ashton	London
Miss Lawrence	..	Greenwood	..	Barnby	..
Marshall	..	Grinling	..	Boardman	Norwich
Metcalf	..	Gunton	..	Britton	..
Morris	..	Hill, H	..	Clare, E	..
Newstead	..	Hill, Horace	..	Creed, J	..
Palmer	..	Hindes	..	Farrer	..
Mrs Peck	..	Hinsby	..	Giffin	London
Miss Roper	..	Ladell	..	Gooch	Norwich
Mrs Rudd	..	Lamb, H	..	Green, W	..
Scarles	..	Lamb, B	..	Harcourt, T. Jun	..
Miss Smith	..	Lane	..	Hill, J F	..
Swann	..	Mann	..	Lawrence	..
Tripp	..	Merry	..	Mann	..
Mrs Trory	..	Middleton	..	Miller	London
Miss Turner, H	..	Newbegin	..	Minns	Norwich
Turner, M A	..	Norman	..	Roberts	..
Wayham	..	Norton	..	Roe, B	..
West	Yarmouth	Olley	..	Roe, W	London
West, S	..	Peck	..	Theobald	Norwich

List of chorus members
Norfolk and Norwich Triennial Festival 1842

FIRST ALTOS.

Thorne	Norwich
White, J. jun.	..
White, T W	..
Woolsey	Yarmouth

SECOND ALTOS.

Mr Burrage	Norwich
Buttifant	..
Buttifant, jun.	..
Darkin	..
Fisk	..
Genge	London
Green C	Norwich
Jones	London
Lanham	Norwich
Larkman	..
Nolloth	Yarmouth
Nolloth, jun.	..
Partridge	Norwich
Perring	London
Raikes	..
Reynolds	Norwich
Rudd, H	..
Sexton, Joseph	..
Sexton, R	..
Skill	..
Smith, H T	..
Tuck	..
Widdows, J	..
Widdows, F	..

FIRST TENORS.

Mr Alger	London
Aldis	Norwich
Amis, D	..
Banham	..
Beevor, W	..
Bray, W	..
Burrage	..
Clare, F	..
Cullyer	..
Day, Rev. G	..
Gooch	..
Goose	..
Green, J	..
Harrison	..
Hayden, T	..
Hayden, W	..
Hill, M	..
Holl	..
Kerrison	..
Lambert	Bradford
Lane	Norwich
Love	..
Manning	..
Metcalf	..
Norfor	Yarmouth
Phillips	Norwich
Rippingham	London

FIRST TENORS.

Sothern, S	Norwich
Sturgess	..
Tripp	..
White	..
Widdows, F	..

SECOND TENORS.

Mr Amis, R	Norwich
Berry, Joseph	..
Bolton, G	..
Brighton	..
Britton	..
Curle	..
Curtis	..
Darley	..
Engledow	..
English	..
Grice	London
Harcourt, A	Norwich
Harcourt, T	..
Hare	..
Hill, John	..
Hoard	..
Liddeman	..
Lovick	..
Nobbs	..
Porter	..
Pye, J	..
Robinson	..
Rudd, W	..
Sadler, J	..
Scarles	..
Sexton, R	..
Smith	..
Sparkall	..
Stevens	..
Sutton	..
Taylor, W	..
Waller, Robert	..
Woodcraft	..

FIRST BASSES.

Mr Armes	Norwich
Berry, John	..
Bond	..
Bowers	Aylsham
Boyce	Norwich
Burgess	..
Campling	..
Cannell	..
Clark	..
Clark, T	..
Field	London
Frier	Norwich
Gedge	..
Gale	Ipswich
Gilbeigh	London
Hall	Norwich
Harcourt, James	..
Hardacre	Hadleigh

FIRST BASSES.

Hill, R	Norwich
Kench	London
Lamb, T	Norwich
Lord	..
Luckett	..
Moore	..
Morter	..
Peck	..
Perry	..
Pigg	..
Priest	..
Sexton, H	..
Sothern, G	..
Syer	..
Tillyard	..
Turner	..
Wade	..
Wade, M	..
Waller, E sen.	..

SECOND BASSES.

Mr Barclay	London
Beevor	Norwich
Berry, James	..
Betts	..
Browne, E	..
Burrell, James	..
Campling	..
Cooke	Ipswich
Creed	Norwich
Farman	..
Farrer	..
Gosling	..
Green	London
Greenwood	Norwich
Guyton	..
Hare, R	..
Hicks, L	..
Holmes	..
Kerrison	..
Lamb, W	..
Novello	London
Pye, A	Norwich
Roe, Bart.	..
Roe, W	..
Rump	..
Rudd	..
Sadler, R	..
Saunders	..
Sexton, G	..
Smith	Bradford
Smith, W	Norwich
Stacey	..
Sugden	Halifax
Tuxford	Norwich
Tuxford, W	..
Waller, E jun.	..
Warnes	..
Wooler	..
Wunderlich	Wurtemburg

CHORUS MASTER—MR. JOHN HILL.

from India by his brother. The audience demonstrated their appreciation with loud applause. A madrigal by Edward Taylor "Sweetheart Why Turn Away Thy Sight" was however not so well received. The "females led" and it was thought to be of great promise until the "males" joined in, their "loudness and coarseness of style destroying all the pleasure of hearing it".

The society's October concert was even less successful. The audience, although not numerous, gave little applause. Mozart's cantata "Let God Arise" was the main work, but the programme was considered rather tame. During the second part people gradually left the hall, needing more enlivening music to induced them to remain until the end.

Friction arose within the society resulting in it being dissolved and reformed. In November 1844 the festival lost its instigator and founder member Richard Bacon who died aged 69 at his Costessey home. His death cast a shadow over the city.

CHAPTER 5

The Death of John Hill

The curious music lover had the opportunity in March 1845 to hear Mr. Richardson's Rock Band at the Assembly House. Richardson, a stone mason from Crostwaite near Keswick in the Lake District, had made a rather novel and ingenious instrument, which he had named a Petrachord, by using stone from Skiddaw. The rock was thought to have a high metal content. For 13 years he carved and shaped stones which he had carried down the mountain on his back. The instrument had 2 rows of stone bars 2 feet long and 2-3 inches broad resting on straw ropes within a wooden frame. They were arranged according to the key of the music to be performed; the lower row always forming a natural scale. Any accidentals were played on the upper row. The instrument required 3 performers each with 2 leather headed wooden hammers to strike the bars.

The genteel audience was astonished by the sound it produced which resembled that of a glass harmonicon. Rossini's overture to the "Barber of Seville" and Richardson's own composition "Waltzes and Galop from Skiddaw" were just 2 of the items performed. The crowded room obviously enjoyed this new sound as several encores were played

Elwin had begun to search for a new conductor for the 1845 festival. Taylor could not oblige. His wife's poor health had necessitated a move to Devonshire. Spohr, Mendelssohn and Costa were all approached before Julius Benedict was finally appointed Festival Conductor. Turle was once again engaged as organist. The festival chorus totalled 272; of whom 42 were women. (in 1824 there had been 7) and only 16 of the singers came from outside Norwich.

Lodgings and residences were full to overflowing as the new railroad brought visitors into the city.

On Tuesday evening the hall took on a "sparkling and comfortable" appearance as the crimson backs to the seats and the ladies brightly coloured dresses glowed in the brilliant gas light. "Alexander's Feast" by Handel was the main work in the programme.

The miscellaneous concert on Thursday evening proved so popular that 200 people had to be turned away. The programme included Benedict's villanella "Strew Joyously".

Julius Benedict

The "Messiah" on Friday morning producing the finest singing throughout the festival. John Hill's skilful training being recognised "...it must be the greatest gratification to him to find his endeavours crowded with the most perfect success. It is his energy and choral tuition that the Norwich Festival is indebted for the glorious choral effect this week exhibited".

In March 1846, John was presented with a £20 gratuity in recognition of his skill and assiduity. A month later in St. Andrew's Hall Elwin was presented with a silver coffee service and a dozen spoons. The coffee pot bore the inscription "Presented to the Rev. Elwin of the Choral Society by the professional and amateurs of music and his personal friends in the acknowledgement of his zeal in promoting the object of the Norfolk and Norwich music festival from its institution in 1834". Elwin found it hard to express his feelings at this moving occasion but said he felt content with the knowledge that after his death the festival would survive.

John Hill then rose and presented Elwin with a scroll containing the names of the 388 subscribers who had generously given £205-0s-7d. Taking this opportunity he paid his own tribute to the man whom he had known since 1824. John recalled with affection how Elwin, a tall, thin, crotchety yet amusing man; used to be able to double himself up inside a pedal pipe. On handing him the scroll John commented that he was sure it would be valued as much as the coffee set, then wished him a long life where hopefully his infirmities would not increase.

Following the presentation members of the choral society dined at the Saloon in Victoria Gardens. Some 220 sat down to an excellent dinner after which toasts were made; one of which being "to John Hill" their "invaluable" chorus master. Their singing of glees, madrigals and songs continued well into the late hours.

During the summer of 1846 John fell ill. Consequently he was unable to instruct the chorus as effectively as he would have wished. It resulted in the chorus not being up to its usual standard for the July concert. Other attractions in the city also contributed to the concert's poor attendance, many of whom took their leave during the final item "Now Tramp" by Bishop.

John Hill died from stomach cancer on 28th July at the age of 48. This man who was described as having a well controlled temper, undeviating modesty and an acute ear, had borne his pain with Christian fortitude. "The loss of this excellent man will be severely felt". He was buried in the family plot* on the Rosary cemetery situated on the right hand side of the most westerly path. The headstone does not bear his name but that of his wife Sarah who had died on 15th June 1845.

*Plot number E No2/660.
1= NRO SO33/2
2= NRO SO33/3
3= Pigot's commercial directory of Norfolk 1822
4= Norfolk Annals p 238 NRO.
5= NRO MS21197
6= NRO SO33/1
7= NRO SO33/4
8 = Pigot's commercial directory of Norfolk 1830
9= NRO SO33/5
10= PRO 1841 census reference 788/10 enumerator schedule 15, page 21.
11= NRO SO33/6
12= Grove's Dictionary of Music and Musicians, 1910 edition.
All other information from the "Norwich Mercury", the "Norfolk Chronicle" and the "Annals of the Norfolk and Norwich Triennial Musical Festivals" by R.H. Legge and W. E. Hansell published by Jarrold in 1896.

PART II
JAMES FREDERICK HILL
CHAPTER 6
Early Life

James Frederick Hill was born on 5th May 1817 in the parish of St. Michael at Thorn. He received his early musical training from his father, John Hill. At the age of 8, James Frederick became a chorister at the cathedral and an apprentice to Buck, staying on a further 2 years after completion to be Buck's assistant. By 1842 he had become a professional music teacher living in Prince's St. (1). In conjunction with his father, he had edited and arranged the "Norwich Tune Book" inserting 14 of his own compositions. This book was recognised in its time, as a valuable collection of psalmody.

After John's death, James Frederick, aged 29, became conductor of the choral society and chorus master of the festival. The first choral concert under his baton in October 1846 presented a selection of music which seldom had been bettered; Macfarren's "Two Merry Gypsies" and airs from Mendelssohn's "St Paul" forming part of the programme.

Although John's death and Elwin's ill health greatly affected the enthusiasm of the choral society, the city did not lack grand musical entertainment in 1847. As Elwin pressed ahead with plans for the 1848 festival by writing to Mendelssohn in the quest for a new oratorio, C. F. Hall (leader of the Drury Lane Theatre) and G. Smith (Norwich's theatre manager) (2) engaged Jenny Lind for a fee of £1000,(2) to give 2 concerts in St. Andrew's Hall during September 1847. It was to be Jenny's first visit to England.

The concert dates of Monday 20th and Wednesday 22nd were agreed but on the 18th it was announced that she had been indisposed with a sore throat and fever since the previous Sunday thus delaying her prior engagement in Scotland. This brought about a hastily revised schedule, the concert of the 20th being rearranged for Thursday 24th. Seats for the concerts cost 2 guineas, 1 guinea and 10/6d and for the first time could be reserved, ensuring everyone would be guaranteed a seat.

It was 8 o'clock on the Tuesday evening when Jenny Lind arrived in the city. Tension had mounted throughout the day as to whether she could fulfil her engagement. As she entered Bishop

Jenny Lind in 1848

Stanley's palace, a joyous peal of bells from St Peter's church heralded her arrival.

Heavy rain fell on Wednesday morning but by evening it was fine. Queues started to form outside St. Andrew's Hall 2 hours before the doors opened. No carts or carriages were allowed to pass the hall whilst the concert was in progress, so barriers were erected across all the roads in the area.

An orchestra comprising of the most eminent members of the Queen's Theatre, the Italian Opera and the Philharmonic Band, under the conductorship of Balfe, had been engaged to accompany her and also Sig. Gardini and Mme and Sig. F. La Blache as supporting artists. The concert commenced with the overture to "Der Freischütz" by Weber. A burst of applause greeted Jenny as she was led forward by Balfe to sing for the first time before an English audience. None of the 1700 present stirred from their seats during the whole concert. She had won their hearts. Thursday's concert brought equal success and Jenny consented to give an extra performance on Saturday at 1 o'clock. The tickets for this concert cost 10/6d or 5/-. 2500 people crowded into the hall. Choristers from the cathedral sat near the orchestra and to their delight Jenny smiled and spoke to them frequently.

After the performance she retired to the chambers of Mr. Lowne, the governor of the workhouse which adjoined the hall. Here she met the children of George Smith. The youngest of whom she sat upon her knee and kissed several times. As she left to enter her carriage the workhouse inmates cheered and waved. The women from the workhouse were often employed to clean the hall after concerts. (3)

Before leaving Norwich, Jenny invited the choristers to take tea with her; the boys managing to devour a large sponge cake. She left on the 6 o'clock train. The platform was full of people waving "Good Bye".

CHAPTER 7

1848 Festival

Mendelssohn replied to Elwin's letter on 7th October 1847. His forthcoming concerts in Germany meant he would be unable to complete his new work, thought to be "Christus", in time for the 1848 festival. Instead he suggested a performance of "Elijah" composed the previous year saying it would give him great pleasure to come to Norwich and conduct the performance himself. A month later, on Thursday the 4th November 1847, at the age of 38, Mendelssohn died.

Elwin's wife died in February 1848. This caused him to retire from the festival and move to Leeds to be with his daughter. He was succeeded by T. D. Eaton.

By July no soloists had been secured for the festival. Jenny Lind had been invited to return to Norwich for the occasion but despite being offered £1000 she could not accept the invitation. Although the prospect looked bleak, the choral society continued to practice regularly. To raise their spirits, 60 of them sat down to tea at Cattermole's Hotel, at Thorpe (5). The property was situated on the river's edge. Among the many toasts which followed their meal was one "To Messrs. Harcourt and Hill the conductors of the instrumental and choral department". The evening slipped away with the singing of glees, solos and duets performed on the piano by Harcourt and Hill. Such good feeling prevailed that the hour was late before they departed.

Pauline Viardot Garcia and Marietta Alboni were eventually engaged in August for a fee of £300 and the 24 year old Castellan for £140. James Frederick had been to London receiving £1-16s-2d for his expenses (4). Several members of the Hill family were taking part in the festival. James Frederick's younger brother, Horace, was playing the oboe. Edward Bunnett, later to become a prominent Norwich musician, sang in the 2nd trebles. James Corps *of Chapelfield had tuned the organ.(4)

On Monday 11th September 1848 the Duke of Cambridge, arrived for the festival on the midday train from London. A large body of citizens greeted him at Trowse. He then travelled by carriage by way of Bracondale, Surrey Rd., Surrey St., Rampant Horse St. and Brigg St. to the Market Place. At the Guildhall he received a presentation from the corporation before continuing his journey to Bishop Stanley's palace.

Tuesday evening's concert commenced with Beethoven's 8th Symphony; the Duke arriving at the close of the first movement. The welcoming applause from the audience brought the band to a halt. After the singing of the National Anthem the symphony was resumed.

Spohr's "Christian Prayer" was performed on Wednesday morning and the evening miscellaneous concert concluded with a "new National Anthem". George Lindley had written the words to the music of William Vincent Wallace. The first performance of this anthem had only recently been given by the Sacred Harmonic Society in Exeter Hall on 26th April. It was heralded as a massive production in the key of C. Every note sounding as if it had been chiselled in rock. "A genius of composition of superior order".

Mendelssohn's "Elijah" was the main attraction on Thursday morning. The work, seen as the last great work before the composer's death, had already been performed in Birmingham, London and Gloucester.

The overjoyed Duke, who frequently referred to the score which laid on his table, called forth "Your choruses are grand", inducing every professional musician present to join in the praise.

The air "Lift Thine Eyes" was repeated following a signal from the gallery and the choruses "Holy God the Lord" and "Then shall your light shine" brought the audience to their feet. Not one person left the hall until the final note had sounded.

Marietta Alboni won her audience on Thursday evening. Until then she had not lived up to expectation. But this much acclaimed contralto, later to be described as "an elephant with a nightingale in her throat" because of her obesity, triumphed gloriously with an aria from Rossini's opera "Semiramide". "Rule Britannia" concluded the concert. The chorus fully entering into the spirit of this national song by bursting into a crescendo for the final phrase "Britons never will be slaves". The word slaves being sung in a manner which evoked considerable laughter from its listeners. At the time there were several small revolutions in Europe which were ruthlessly put down.

The festival concerts were always of considerable length. On Friday morning "Davidde Penitente" by Mozart was performed in its entirety. It was followed by Handel's "Israel in Egypt". Those eager to leave as the concert drew towards its conclusion missed the delayed signal for a repeat of the final chorus. Castellan had left the orchestra: the chorus had put aside their music. Resuming their positions Benedict signalled to begin. The first note arrested the departure and many who had already quitted the hall tried to return.

With the hall full of people standing everywhere, drinking in the last of the gorgeous harmonies, the musical festival of 1848 drew to a close.

* Corps advertised himself as tuner of the organs in Norwich and Winchester cathedrals. He had moved from London where he had worked for 23 years and had 18 years experience with the late establishment of Flight and Robson. His address later became Crescent Rd, Norwich before he returned to London in 1851 to premises at 16 Pleasant Row, Pentonville Hill. In Norfolk he had built organs in the churches of Yaxham, Necton, Barnham Broom, Felthorpe, St. Mark's Lakenham, St. Michael at Thorn and a large instrument for Witton vicarage near North Walsham.

CHAPTER 8

Jenny Lind

The choral society wasted little time before arranging their next concert, a performance of the "Messiah" given in St. Andrew's Hall on 5th January 1849. To encourage people to come it was made known that should the weather prove unfavourable the hall would be heated by stoves. Admission prices were kept to the minimum. A single ticket was just 3/- and a subscription ticket either 1 guinea or 12/6d, this giving 4 or 2 transferable tickets to each concert in the series. 230 people took advantage of the saving and registered as subscribers.

Due to the length of the oratorio it commenced at 7.30pm with the doors opening the usual 1 hour in advance. As 1300 people approached the hall the streets took on the appearance of a festival evening. The performance was "sublime" with all the 300 performers doing justice to the work, except for Mr. Seguin whose voice did not possess enough power to fill the hall. When the concert drew to a close the waiting carriages stretch back into the Market Place.

Under the care and ability of James Frederick, the Norwich Choral Society had regained their former esteem.

Just 2 weeks later the city was engulfed in a wave of excitement. Jenny Lind was returning to St. Andrew's Hall to give 2 gratuitous concerts. Her visit created a sense of euphoria throughout the city.

On Saturday 20th January 1849 the mayor's carriage awaited her arrival on the 5 o'clock train. As it drew into the station the gates were opened and a rush of people flooded onto the platform. They cheered heartily as the mayor escorted her to his carriage and Jenny waved her handkerchief as she was driven off towards the Bishop's palace.

In the evening church bells rang in her honour. Selected company gathered at the palace and before she would sing Jenny requested that the servants be summoned upstairs.

On Sunday she attended morning worship at the cathedral. Many thought she might sing during the service and therefore the congregation was much larger than usual. To their disappointment her voice was not heard.

At the palace on Monday, Jenny gave audience to several Norwich manufacturers who had brought along specimens of their work which they begged her to accept. Mr. Sultzer of St.

Augustine's presented her with a rich violet satin dress which she agreed to wear at the Tuesday morning concert. Mr. Willett presented a dress made of new material which, by permission, had been named Lindianna crape, in her honour. Several other dresses were also graciously received.

Monday's concert commenced at 8pm. Tickets costing 10/6d, 7/6d, or 5/- could be purchased from an office situated in the entrance of the Government School of Design, opposite the glass shop of Messrs. Lovicks & Co in St Andrew's Broad Street. The 10/6d tickets were by reservation only and showed a section letter and seat number; the sections within the hall being indicated by large placards bearing the letters A-F. The system worked most efficiently. A small orchestra, constructed at the east end allowed the large west end orchestra to be allocated to the audience.

The concert opened with the overture from Hérold's "Zampa". The mayor then led Jenny onto the orchestra. The audience rose, their cheering, clapping and shouts of "Bravo" lasting for many minutes. Accompanied by the band Jenny sang the first and last verses of the National Anthem; the second verse being sung by the supporting vocalists Miss Dolby, Sig. Marras and Sig. Belletti. A burst of applause erupted at the end of each verse. Few had heard Jenny sing in English. (In 1847 her knowledge of the language had been limited) but her rich mellifluous voice, clear, distinct and "voluptuously bell like" filled the hall.

Tuesday morning was dull and cloudy but, at noon, as the second concert was about to begin, the sun broke through, casting its rays upon those assembled inside the hall. The programme, mostly of sacred music, included a performance of "Lift Thine Eyes" from "Elijah" sung by Master Bunnett, Miss Dolby and Jenny Lind. Throughout the concert the custom of listening to sacred music in silence was constantly violated, the audience being unable to contain their excitement.

As Jenny came to the close of her final song a placard was hoisted in the orchestra bearing the words "Three cheers for Jenny Lind". It received a prompt response. After the concluding overture from "Zauberflöte" a further 3 cheers were raised, this time to the conductor Julius Benedict.

Jenny left the hall by way of the workhouse courtyard. Here she encountered the children of the inmates, to whom she spoke kindly in passing. At her request the children, together with the scholars from the Blind School, had been placed under the galleries in the hall, so they could listen to the concert unobserved.

People lined the streets, shouting "Hurrah" as her carriage passed on its way to the Bishop's palace.

On Wednesday morning a scroll was presented to Jenny by her host in recognition of her charitable deeds. The ladies and gentlemen assembled at the palace listened to the Bishop's touching complimentary address and watched their Prima Donna's emotions spill over into tears which trickled down her face. Grasping the Bishop's hand, Jenny kissed it.

Later that day she toured the manufactories where her gifts had been made. At Mr. Sultzer's premises she expressed a wish to see the man who had woven her violet satin dress. The weaver was summoned and shaking his hand, she thanked him saying she hoped he would always be in full employment.

Receipts from the 2 concerts totalled £1859-11s-0d. After expenses over £1250 remained for charitable purposes.

Initially it was intended to use the money to convert a disused malthouse in St. Stephen's into a public baths and wash room but this proved too expensive. Instead a house in Pottergate was purchased and adapted to an infirmary for sick children. It opened on 12th June 1853.

CHAPTER 9

Choral Society Concerts of 1849 and 1850

The choral society held their annual convivial meeting in June 1849 at Cattermole's Hotel. Some arrived on the steam packet Victoria and others by road. At 6 o'clock 170 members sat down to tea at 2 long tables which extended the full length of the room. The meal concluded with the singing of the canon "Non Nobis Domine". They then adjourned to the gardens for an hour, amusing themselves until the tables were cleared. On returning, Mr. Eaton took his place at the head of the table He spoke of how he had hesitantly accepted the presidency of the society after Elwin's resignation, but had been warmly received and his duties light. He concluded his speech by saying how he hoped the society would continue to be a credit to the city. Glasses were then raised and 3 cheers were repeated thrice, to Mr. Eaton. Toasts to the health of Mr. Hill the chorus master and Mr. Harcourt the instrumental conductor were also drunk before this most agreeable evening came to an end, it being past midnight.

Rehearsals started the following Monday for the second choral society concert of 1849; a performance of "Judas Maccabaeus". Their first concert, Haydn's "Creation" on March 29th, had been over shadowed by the murder trial of James Rush.

In this second concert cathedral choristers Master Mann and Master Bunnett were billed to be soloists. However Bunnett had to withdraw because his voice had broken. He was replaced by Master Gaul who appeared somewhat frightened by the ordeal which detracted from his singing. Miss Henderson's voice was also regrettable, a lisp affecting her pronunciation.

Under the training of James Frederick the choral concerts continued in 1850 with "Elijah" on 4th April, a miscellany of choruses and madrigals on 29th July and Handel's "Samson" on 17th October. This was to be their last concert before the 1851 festival and it drew an enormous crowd. The hall was a mass of happy faces from the base of the organ to the most eastern extremities of the edifice. A most delightful sight.

The chorus and band had been arranged differently to previous occasions; both being situated on the nave section of the orchestra which was extended forward about 3 feet to accommodate. In the past the instrumentalists had occupied the nave part of the orchestra and the chorus the north and south wings in the aisles. But the wings were now filled by those unable to obtain a seat in the main body of the hall. In this new arrangement the principal singers took the front row seats of the orchestra. On each side and behind were the trebles. The tenors and basses to their north and the altos to the south with the band in the centre of the chorus. The voices and instruments blended well, filling the hall with one tremendous unified sound. The effect was magnificent, exceeding all the society's previous performances.

By 1851 James Frederick had moved from Prince's St and was living at 46 Pottergate St. with his wife Laura Norton, 5 years his junior, their 2 sons Frederick and Theodore and young daughter Edith. They employed a servant Elizabeth Haines. (6)

From October 1850 until June 1851 Mr. Thomas Fisher advertised pianos, seraphines and organs for sale from this address.

On 27th March 1851 James Frederick played the organ at a concert given by the band of the 11th Hussars, the Philharmonic Band and the Glee Party. The highlight of the evening was an astonishing feat by Mr. Sprake, the bandmaster, who played 7 different wind instruments in a concert piece written by Brepsant. The Hussars received praise for their exemplary behaviour throughout the evening.

In April the festival committee decided to postpone the festival until 1852. The Great Exhibition at the Crystal Palace was drawing people to London. The best singers had been engaged by the Opera House and Her Majesty's Theatre; both having extended their season, and Julius Benedict was touring the United States with Jenny Lind.

CHAPTER 10

Bexfield versus Pierson

A new oratorio "Israel Restored" by William Bexfield was presented to the choral society committee in the Old Library Room of St. Andrew's Hall in May 1851. The young composer played most of the work through on the piano.

Bexfield was born in Norwich on 27th April 1824. At the age of 7 he became a pupil of Buck. By the age of 11 he had composed an 8 part anthem. He took up the position of organist at Boston church and married the daughter of Mr. Millington, a local solicitor. During 1851 he was appointed organist at St. Helen's, Bishopgate, London being selected from 35 applicants. Mendelssohn thought most highly of this young man's talent.

The composer's masterly piano playing delighted everyone present. The bass part was sung by Mr. Metcalfe, the tenor part by Mr. English and 3 choristers from the cathedral sang the treble line. The boys had only seen the score the previous day but sang with such accuracy and effect that expressions of commendation were frequently called forth. The first public performance of the oratorio was given by the choral society under the leadership of James Frederick, in St. Andrew's Hall on Thursday 16th October 1851, starting at 7 o'clock. The band was augmented for the occasion, bringing the total number of performers to 350. The pitch of the organ had been altered to that of the wind instruments. Bexfield conducted a most creditable performance in the presence of 1815 people who had paid 3/- admission.

On the evening of Thursday 10th January 1852, the choral society gave a performance of the "Messiah" with Mozart's accompaniment which had now become the custom. Amongst the 350 performers was Mr. Sprake, playing the clarionet. The band was more "scarce" than one would have desired but this was usual. An unlucky bassoon popped out a note in the wrong place occasionally and a fiddle adventurously wandered from its desired path, but this did not dampen their enthusiasm. The choruses went well and expressions of joy could be seen on the faces of everyone present. Some of the subscribers had been displeased over the allocation of the reserved seats and expressed their feelings in the local press. They wanted first choice of the seats. The practice of selling tickets in bulk to single applicants was also condemned. Mr. Eaton replied stating no more than 8 tickets had been sold to any one person and that the main problem simply was that the building was too small to accommodate everyone in comfort. "Give us a music hall capable of holding 3000, we can not do as other places whilst we are cabin'd, cribb'd and confin'd".

The next choral concert on 20th March reported no seating problems. The following week James Frederick and chorus members met in the "new" room at the Royal Hotel to celebrate the success of their concert series. It had made a profit of £170 for society funds. Their songs during this evening of jollification were accompanied by Mr. Howlett's band. The society was regarded as being entirely devoted to the art of music for only 7 out of their 300 members received some form of remuneration.

Henry Hugo Pierson was a guest at this meeting. He was visiting Norwich to try and persuade its musical gentlemen that his new oratorio "Jerusalem" was worthy of receiving its first performance in the forthcoming festival.

Pierson, at that time, was a lecturer at Edinburgh University. He had been born Henry Hugh Pearson the son of the Dean of Salisbury but had changed his name whilst living in Germany. So keen was Henry to have his work performed that he wrote to his brother the Rector of Guildford asking if the curate at Guildford would send a letter to his father, George V. Cox, outlining the merits of the oratorio. George, being a respected gentleman, was then expected to contact someone of influence within the festival circle. (7) In mid April a private performance of part of "Jerusalem" was given to a selected audience of 300 in the Assembly Room by the choral society, the philharmonic band and the cathedral choristers. Among those present were the Bishop of Norwich and the Dean. At its conclusion the work was deemed worthy of a place in festival, as an offer of £1000 had been made should any loss be incurred. Dr. Bexfield was also anxious to have his oratorio "Israel Restored" performed in the festival. Both had their own supporters and a rivalry developed as to which work was the best. Pierson expressed his concern. He did not want to appear an opponent of Bexfield, saying he would "exert himself to the utmost" not to exclude Dr. Bexfield from the festival. He would even consider withdrawing if there was assurance that "Israel Restored" would take his place. But the best solution he felt was to include both works (7). Bexfield's work was accepted for the festival.

During August Pierson returned to assist with the rehearsals of "Jerusalem" and found himself most satisfied with the ability and zeal displayed by the choral society. Rehearsals of both "Jerusalem" and "Israel Restored" had taken place in the Hanover Square rooms, London for the metropolitan faction of the chorus, James Frederick receiving £2-2s-0d (8) for his attendance. Bexfield had been present to conduct his own work but Pierson entrusted the conducting of "Jerusalem" to Benedict. Both works were in print before the festival; "Jerusalem" being published by Novello. Mr. Howlett's shop in London St, Norwich advertised a piano edition for 31/-. Copies of "Israel Restored" were advertised as being available from the composer for 25/- with a reduction of 4/- to Norwich Choral Society members. After the festival the price of this work was to be increase to one and half guineas.

The first full rehearsals took place on the Monday before the festival in St. Andrew's Hall. Visual improvements had been made to the buildings interior by covering the passage entrances under the orchestra with glazed calico drapes supplied by Messrs. Clarke and Hunter. At 10am Benedict was ready to commence but it was 10.30am before a sufficient number of performers had arrived. All day they concentrated on "Jerusalem"; many of the choruses proving both elaborate and difficult. The hall had to be vacated in the evening to make way for the last promenade concert so Mendelssohn's "Midsummer Night's Dream" was rehearsed in the Assembly Rooms. Tuesday morning brought torrential rain. Young Dr. Bexfield's work, Henry Leslie's anthem "Let God Arise" and a selection from the coming evening's miscellaneous programme were worked upon. The rain continued all day. Special trains brought masses of visitors into the city for the evening concert. The usual starting time had been brought forward half an hour to accommodate the expected length of the programme. At 5 o'clock people began to arrive at the hall, sheltering from the rain under the boarded entrance of the Great South door. "Midsummer Night's Dream" formed the second part of the concert with Mrs Fanny Keeble reading Shakespeare's play accompanied by Mendelssohn's incidental music. After the overture her voice rang out through the hall for the next hour varying according to the characters but as she tired her performance became wearisome. By 11 o'clock the galleries had become almost deserted and it was nearly midnight before she read Puck's last valediction.

On Wednesday morning the hall was thinly populated. Few had come to hear Leslie's anthem and Bexfield's oratorio but a most perfect stillness fell over the hall as they listened in earnest to the oratorio's 18 beautiful choruses which never strayed from the rules of harmony. During the chorus "Marvellous are Thy Works", the audience rose and contrary to the customary silence, applauded. The Bishop, the instrumentalists and all the soloists joining in the salutations.

The concert concluded with the "Dead March" as a tribute to the late Duke of Wellington. A few days earlier a muffled toll of bells had rung out across the city for several hours, to mark the news of his death.

The audience Wednesday evening for the miscellaneous concert was also small. A selection from Benedict's opera the "Minnesinger" was the principal work; this being its first performance and thought yet unpublished.

The attendance recovered on Thursday morning as 1400 came to hear "Jerusalem". This lengthy composition lasting 4½ hours, had 47 divisions of which 27 were choral and 18 songs. The libretto had been written by W. Sancroft Holmes, a friend of the composer, who resided at Gawdy Hall near Harleston. The work had been dedicated to the Archbishop of Canterbury. It was totally different in character to anything heard before and the audience sat spellbound until the end. Pierson was called to come forward again and again but he bowed politely from a chair at the back of the hall. Eventually he conceded and was led onto the platform by Benedict. The audience cried out for a speech but he was too emotional to oblige so Benedict spoke on his behalf. In the evening the finale from Mendelssohn's incomplete opera "Lorely" was given for the first time in Norwich and a song "Gloomy and dim the eventful morning broke", written by Macfarren, was sung in memory of the Duke of Wellington. Those who had been at Wednesday morning's concert had received a leaflet informing them of the song's inclusion in Thursday's programme. Unfortunately those who had not seen the leaflet were at a total loss as to what was happening and the incident passed off quietly. The hands of the clock had crept past midnight before the concert finally ended.

On Friday morning the hall was packed to capacity to hear the a most perfect performance of the "Messiah". Hundreds stood in the passages along the galleries and others climbed up ladders into the roof. Hundreds more were turned away.

As soon as the oratorio finished carpenters, waiting in the wings invaded the hall and started dismantling the galleries in readiness for the evening ball which still concluded the festival. These structures, which had taken days to erect disappeared within an hour. By 10 o'clock 450 persons from eminent families began their evening of dancing, refreshing themselves with tea, coffee, negus and fruit supplied by Messrs. Clarke and Hunter. 400 spectators occupied the great orchestra paying 2/6d for the privilege. It was 4.30 on Saturday morning before the company finally dispersed. A total of 6610 people had visited the festival. The choral society had attended 65 rehearsals and having now relinquished their local dialect their words were both clear and round. In "Jerusalem" the soprani reached C altissimo, and their performance in this piece alone made them worthy of their high reputation, the whole chorus singing with amazing earnestness and precision.

"Mr. James Frederick Hill has reason to be proud of his excellent troop".

However certain factions of society fiercely attacked Pierson's "Jerusalem". His style, likened to that of Wagner, infringed on all the rules of harmony and counterpoint. "Not a single phrase closed in the ordinary way causing incessant torment to the ear with startling modulations". "Voices were abused by being called to sing the most desperate intervals". "Like Frankenstein he had given the world a monstrous creation". On the other side, those in support of the work commented that it had affected the 1400 listeners so greatly some had been moved to tears.

Henry Leslie was most satisfied with the near perfect performance of his anthem on the Wednesday morning. His gratitude being endorsed by a £3 donation to the choral society and a copy of the score.

The funeral of the Duke of Wellington took place in St Paul's Cathedral in November. As a mark of respect all the shops in Norwich closed. A detachment of the finest singers from Norwich and Ely strengthened the choir. One of whom was a Mr. Hill.

CHAPTER 11

Death of Bexfield.

Spohr's oratorio the "Fall of Babylon" was chosen for the choral society's first concert of 1853. It was sung with great precision and effect, James Frederick receiving high praise for their splendid performance.

2 months later a large party from Norwich travelled to Exeter Hall, London to hear a performance of Pierson's "Jerusalem".

In July 1853, the choral society performed Haydn's "Creation". Their previous high standard being well maintained. But the instrumentalists started badly. Their rendition of "Chaos" being far from effective.

The 27th July found the choral society enjoying their triennial treat bestowed upon them by the festival committee in gratitude of their festival contribution. Instead of the usual visit to Mrs. Cattermole's Hotel, some 200 members took the early morning train to Lowestoft. The tickets for the excursion being presented by railway entrepreneur Morton Peto. After an hour's rest to recover from the journey they proceeded to the site of the new church of St. John* on the corner of London Rd. South in South Lowestoft. Here they stood and sung the "hallelujah" chorus as part of the ceremony for the laying of the foundation stone by Henry Gurney. The formalities concluded, the party were free to amused themselves until 2.30pm when they partook of an excellent cold dinner in a booth to the front of the Suffolk Hotel. Mr. Eaton took his position at the head of the table with James Frederick Hill and "Mr. Hill" heading the side tables. After the singing of "Non Nobis Domini" the usual toasts were drunk including one to the health of James Frederick. The remainder of the day was spent in the pursuit of various activities. Some ventured on to the bowling green where the sweet sounds of a band could be heard. Others strolled along the pier and the shore while the more adventurous set out to sea on Mr. Lucas' yacht which had been kindly placed, along with its crew, at their disposal for the day. When the railway bell signalled the imminent departure of the last train, the party reluctantly made their way to the station and were returned safely to the city by 10.30pm.

The year's final choral society concert in October was compiled of miscellaneous works. As usual St Andrew's Hall was full. Henry Hugo Pierson's "Roman Dirge" formed part of the programme.

St. John's Church, Lowestoft

This solemn work was felt inappropriate for the occasion. The solo part should have been taken by Mrs. Sims Reeves but at short notice she refused to sing declaring the work unsuitable for the range of her voice. Mrs. Hill bravely stepped in to save the day and with little time to rehearse "exerted herself to do justice to this short but difficult part". Although Mr. Sims Reeves sang his allotted songs well, it was said of his wife that she would never occupy a high position, her voice being "far from good". The concert also featured some most regrettable renditions of songs by Mr. Smith, the lyrics proving far more suited to the tea gardens or the cheap theatre. Their vulgar allusions, enhanced by his buffoonery, were considered quite inappropriate for the occasion.

On October 28th 1853 Bexfield died aged just 29 years. He had suffered from a painful internal disorder for some time. A benefit concert for his widow and 2 children was given in St. Andrew's Hall in December. Despite the extreme severity of the weather it drew one of the largest assemblages of city and county families seen for some time. Mr. W. G. Cusins, the Queen's organist, presided at the organ and the principal instrumentalist came from Her Majesty's private chamber band. Works by Bexfield were included in the programme. 2000 people paid either 10/6d or 5/- admission and a surplus of £500 was given to Mrs. Bexfield.

Plans were now well advanced for the 1854 festival which was to commence on the Tuesday after the first full moon in September. The main reason for a 2 year interval instead of the usual 3 was to avoid the Birmingham festival. Jenny Lind, now married to Otto Goldschmidt, was offered £1500 to appear. She was most anxious to accept, but on the advice of her private physician she finally declined. Little time was left to secure a replacement, however Clara Novello agreed to take part for a fee of £300. Clara had visited Norwich in 1836 for the opening of the Roman Catholic chapel but had never before sung in the festival.

By August cholera was rife in London. People were reluctant to travel for fear of spreading the disease. Britain was involved in the Crimean war and income tax had risen. The exceptionally dry summer had also caused much sickness in the city. James Frederick had moved house and was now living in St. Giles' Terrace. (9)

In a bid to tempt people to the festival ticket prices were reduced and the galleries in the hall constructed to a new plan by the city surveyor, enabling almost everyone to see the solo performers.

The festival was patronised by the new Duke of Wellington who arrived on the Tuesday and was the guest of Samuel Bignold. It had been hoped the bronze statue of the late Duke could be unveiled during his visit but as the granite pedestal was incomplete, the ceremony had to be postponed. However the bronze was on public display, with viewing allowed by ticket only.

For the first time an additional concert was given on the Tuesday morning. The weather was bright and warm as the audience listened to Rossini's "Stabat Mater". In the evening Handel's "Acis and Galatea" with Mozart's accompaniment was performed for the first time in Norwich.

The programme Wednesday morning was of great length, comprising of Beethoven's Mass in C and Haydn's "Creation". This time the "Chaos", went well. The absence of works by Haydn in the 1852 festival had met with severe criticism.

A performance of "Elijah" took place on Thursday morning. The audience sat in wonderment as they listened to Elijah's solo asking for rain. A dark cloud suddenly filtered out the sun's rays which had been streaming through the hall windows and the sound of rain, the first for many, many weeks could be heard splashing on the roof.

In the evening Clara Novello caused quite a commotion when she flatly refused to repeat one of her ballads, after being indicated to do so by Benedict. It was unheard of for a performer to refuse but Clara was feeling the strain of the festival.

The public's disappointment was short lived for on Friday morning her singing in the "Messiah" was superb; equal to that of Jenny Lind. The musical skills of Mr. Zeiss, the trumpeter however were not so good, his playing ruining "The Trumpet Shall Sound". The committee were criticised for failing to secure the services of Harper Jnr., but his terms were above those offered.

Due to so many requests for repeats the performance did not conclude until 4 o'clock in the afternoon.

The Friday evening ball this time was held in the Assembly Rooms to avoid the expense of laying down the special flooring needed in St Andrew's Hall. Two rooms were used with a band in each. The attendance dropped dramatically from the usual 500 to only 198. There was ample space for dancing which continued until 4 o'clock in the morning.

The festival made a loss of £103-9s-5d. The deficit being recovered by donations from noblemen and gentlemen. The greatest loss though, was to the charities who usually benefited from the festival's success. To compensate for this, 2 charity concerts were given in October by the festival chorus. With an admission charge of 4/- and 1/- these were well supported.

* St John's church was built by Lucas Bros. and was demolished in 1977.

CHAPTER 12

"Eli"

The choral society, under the baton of James Frederick, gave a performance of the "Messiah" on Friday 5th January 1855, in aid of the "Patriotic Fund". All the performers giving their services gratuitously, even the gas company allowed the free use of gas to light St. Andrew's Hall which would have incurred a cost of between £7 and £8. The audience, who paid either 3/- or 2/- admission were delighted with the performance; Master Atkinson of the cathedral choir having sung 2 solo airs with an intensity of feeling far beyond his years.

In March the choral society's first concert of the series was postponed due to the severity of the weather and did not take place until 1st June when a performance of C. Horsley's oratorio "David" was given, conducted by the composer. James Frederick had been drilling the chorus for the past 4 to 5 months and they sang their parts admirably. The band though was not always in time and frequently proved distressingly "painful to the eye and ear". Their accompaniment to the "Mendelssohnian" airs was "quite at sea". Never before, in Norwich, had an oratorio been so badly performed, the fine choruses being its only redeeming feature.

The second concert on 28th July featured Beethoven's Mass in C and Spohr's "The Last Judgement". Considering the difficulty of the latter work the chorus showed a high standard of excellence.

On the 10th September news reached the city of the fall of Sevastopol. Thousands of people gathered in the Market Place singing the National Anthem and "Rule Britannia". Bands played, the bells of St. Peter Mancroft rang and a bonfire with fireworks on Castle Meadow added to the celebrations. (2)

In October the reputation of the choral society was restored when Clara Novello was engaged for their third concert of the series. Some 1300 people came to hear this lady, described as the finest oratorio singer in England, sing some of her favourite airs. She was in excellent voice.

Jenny Lind returned to Norwich in February 1856 to appear in a performance of the "Messiah" and a miscellaneous concert. A band from London was engaged, strengthened by talented local musicians, one of whom was a Mr. Hill. Benedict conducted.

To avoid the characteristic overcrowding of St. Andrew's Hall,

Jenny Lind 1856

the sale of tickets was limited to the number the hall could comfortably accommodate.

On the afternoon of Monday February 4th the bells of St. Peter Mancroft rang out merrily pending Jenny's arrival then "fired" at the moment the Eastern Union Line train was due to steam into the platform. The train was late and when Jenny arrive the bells were mute. As she alighted from the train accompanied by her husband Otto, the concourse assembled to greet her were also mute. Not a single cheer went up and they stared in silence as the couple were escorted to the awaiting carriage which then conveyed them to Jenny's private apartment at Mr. Allcock's establishment in Queen St.

The chief constable with a sufficient body of police was on duty Tuesday morning to ensured no overcrowding occurred, but the noon performance of the "Messiah" attracted an attendance of only 1000 - 1500. Members of the choral society had even received complimentary tickets for their friends, as a gesture of appreciation for their assistance.

It was obvious from her appearance that Jenny was in delicate health. Her voice had a huskiness in the lower notes which was thought to relate to her medical condition. The mayor called for a repeat of the air "Come Unto Him" to which she complied. It was the only repeat for she indicated to Benedict that her health would not allow any further requests. The concert concluded at 3.30pm. Jenny mustered sufficient strength to sing several solos during Thursday evening's miscellaneous concert, one being "Recueil de Mazourkas de F. Chopin", an arrangement for voice and piano by Otto of some of Chopin's piano works. During the evening Otto also played 2 piano solos. This 3½ hour concert was attended by some 3000 people. Receipts from the 2 performances totalled £2400 with £354 being given to the Jenny Lind Infirmary Account.

The signing of the Peace Treaty on 30th March called for further celebration in the Market Place. Again the bells of St. Peter Mancroft rang out and a bonfire was lit. But this time the fire was in the Market Place which contravened police regulations and was extinguished. Their actions enflamed the revellers who broke windows in protest. Moving on to Castle Meadow the rioters threw a squib under a wagon of straw, then stoned the firemen who came to put out the flames. (2)

After a performance in April of "Elijah" with Clara Novello taking a solo part, the society started rehearsing Costa's oratorio "Eli" for their next concert which customarily was given in the summer assize week. It was Costa's first sacred work and had been performed at the Birmingham festival the previous year.

Soon James Frederick and the choral society found themselves fighting a battle for survival. Mr. Gedge, who had been responsible for the Jenny Lind concerts, was determined to destroy the choral society and the festival. He and his supporters claimed there was no longer a need for local amateur concerts, as people could easily travel by train to the metropolis to hear professionals. The festival was branded antiquated and a bore which should be superseded by 2 grand concerts per annum.

Michael Costa

When the choral society applied to the council for the use of St. Andrew's Hall for their performance of "Eli" in the summer assize week, they found the mayor, Mr. Johnson, had already promised the hall to Mr. Gedge. Gedge was promoting his own performance of "Eli" under the personal direction of Costa, during that very same week. The choral society sent a memorial to the council begging the City Committee to grant them the use of the hall for just one evening. At a subsequent meeting, Councillor Kerrison moved that the society be granted their wish but an amendment was put forward by Mr. Pyman and seconded by Mr. Bullard stating the committee regrettably could not comply with the society's request. A vote was taken on the amendment. It was rejected by 8 votes to 5. (10)

Gedge refused to recognise the City Committee's decision insisting he was entitled to use the hall the entire week. Mr. Eaton sent another note to the Council informing them of Gedge's obstinacy and the Committee's attention was drawn to an advertisement billing Gedge's concert for Wednesday 23rd July. They therefore granted the society use of the hall on Friday 25th, Gedge being instructed to remove the gallery erected for his performance by 4 o' clock on Thursday 24th (10).

The whole affair prompted many persons to write to the press but by the end of June the society had won their case, for Mr Gedge announced the postponement of "Eli" under his promotion. Cllr. Kerrison then recommended to the City Committee that the choral society be granted the use of St. Andrew's Hall on Wednesday 23rd July for their performance of the work (10).

On the morning of the 23rd Howlett's shop was crowded with people wishing to purchase tickets for the choral society's "Eli" under the conductorship of James Frederick Hill.

The audience heard Costa's "weak" choruses sung with "vigour and oneness,"..."little short of marvellous", but the effect of the grand concluding hallelujah chorus was marred by the vast concourse leaving the hall. The performance was still declared a success. Those who had been of the opinion that an amateur chorus could not do justice to this difficult work had been proved wrong. The choral society wanted to show their appreciation to their president, Mr. Eaton, for his part in saving the society from extinction so a subscription fund was set up. The great generosity of members and friends soon resulted in a considerable sum of money being collected. Just 2 weeks after the society's October concert of miscellaneous works which had given universal satisfaction, 200 members and friends gathered in the Lecture Room of St. Andrew's Hall for Mr. Eaton's testimonial. Hugo Pierson was among those present. He marked the occasion by writing a drinking song for tenor and chorus, dedicating the composition to Mr. Eaton.

The Rev. George Day, the eldest member of the society was given the honour of presenting a massive, elegant silver stuff box and silver ink stand purchased from Rossi in the Market Place, to the president. In his speech Day alluded to Mr. Eaton's good temper, forbearance and ability in handling the affairs of the last few months.

It was the first time the female members of the society had attended a social function and after the formalities the ladies entertained the party with solos and part songs arranged by James Frederick especially for the occasion. Their voices had rarely been heard in this manner and the singing of Miss Booth, Miss Livock, Miss Belton, Miss Leech and Miss Ralph equalled that of some of the London professionals who had been engaged in the past.

It was well into the night before the company dispersed.

CHAPTER 13

The Last Festival ?

A cloud of uncertainty hung over the festival. Attendances had been dwindling since the coming of the railway in 1845. It was feared that if concerts fell under the control of private speculators, they would be abandoned once they ceased to be a profitable venture, leaving the city unable to regain its high amateur status.

With this thought in mind the festival committee decided to hold just one more festival to gage the public's opinion.

Leslie's biblical cantata "Judith" and Reinthaler's oratorio "Jephtha and his Daughter" were submitted to the committee for consideration. The cantatas "May Day" by Macfarren and "Robin Hood" by Hatton were also put forward. All were refused. The committee invited Pierson to compose a new work but he declined, stating he was too old but he strongly recommended the German soprano Mme. Leonhardi as one of the festival's solo performers. She had never sung in England before; a fee of £100 was agreed. The opera singer Piccolomini and Clara Novello were also engaged.

As preparations continued for the Norwich Festival, thousands upon thousands of people flocked to the Crystal Palace at Sydenham. This gigantic glass structure was the venue for the first Handel Festival. The event being a grand rehearsal for a magnificent festival planned to commemorate the centenary of Handel's death in 1859. Gray and Davison had constructed a huge organ weighing 20 tons. A band of some 400 excellent musicians and a chorus of 2000 of the finest voices in the Kingdom, including a contingent from Norwich, were formed under the supervision of the Sacred Harmonic Society and the conductorship of Michael Costa. This 5 day festival was a tremendous success.

In Norwich, a new moveable orchestra was under construction from a plan drawn up by the city surveyor, Mr. Benest. The elliptical structure had the performers entrance in the centre. At the final rehearsal the chorus appeared to be huddled together and were unable to hear their own voices above the instrumentalists situated immediately behind them.

The first concert of the festival on Tuesday evening opened with the overture "Ruy Blas" by Mendelssohn followed by the National Anthem. Piccolomini then sang "Batti, Batti" from "Don Giovanni". Her acting ability was greater than that of her singing, but her grace and charm captivated the audience, rendering them deaf to her vocal imperfections. The evening's programme also included Howard Glover's cantata "Tam O Shanter". It was the first time the work had been performed in Norwich.

Mozart's "Requiem" without Edward Taylor's alterations, was given on Wednesday morning. It formed the final work of the concert, having been preceded by the sacred cantata "God Thou Art Great" by Spohr and Mendelssohn's "Hymn of Praise".

As people arrived on Thursday morning they found a notice placed upon every seat informing them of Mme. Leonhardi refusal to sing in that morning's performance of "The Seasons" and in Friday's "Messiah". She felt her acquaintance with the English language inadequate to do justice to the works. Mme. Weiss kindly consented to undertake her part. "The Seasons" was preceded by Beethoven's oratorio "Mount of Olives" which had been arranged by Smart.

The miscellaneous concert in the evening opened with Spohr's symphony "The Seasons" again this work had not been previously performed in Norwich. The attendance was less than usual. A large portion of the concert was devoted to a selection from Pierson's "Faust". For an hour and a half the audience listened to "dreary and dull" music which conveyed many into the "balmy oblivion of sleep". At its conclusion only a few personal friends seated near the orchestra removed their gloves and clapped loudly. A few more in the 5/- gallery stamped their feet but they failed to arouse an enthusiastic response.

The Friday evening ball had always been in fancy dress but this time it was optional. Only 20 of the 400 in attendance kept up the custom.

The festival had made a profit of £351, attracting 120 more visitors than in 1852. The sum of £195 was given to charity and the remainder held in reserve. James Frederick was awarded £42 in addition to his fee for his valuable service throughout the festival.

At a subsequent meeting it was agreed to continue the festival triennially.

The chorus master had little time to recuperate from the strains and stresses of the festival, for on October 20th he conducted a choral society miscellaneous concert in "aid of the fund for the relief of the suffers from the mutinies in India". It was rather too soon after the festival for the chorus to do justice to the works and the small band of instrumentalists looked rather sparse on the new orchestra. There was little, if any, profit made for the fund.

A further recognition of James Frederick's services to music was made in January 1858, this time in the form of a testimonial. On the evening of Monday 18th, 200 members and friends of the Choral Society gathered in the large room at the Royal Hotel for the presentation of a purse of money and a gold watch to their master.

After a meagre and insufficient tea a lively evening of music commenced. The usual toasts were proposed, each being endorsed by the singing of an appropriate glee.

Messrs. Kerrison and Morgan were among those present. Their virtues being praised in a speech by Mr. Eaton. Kerrison, in reply to the glowing tribute paid to him, said he was of the opinion that the success of the late festival was largely due to the labours of the choral body. Their "cultivation of music of a high character not only tended to elevate their minds but also prevented them from indulging in debasing pursuits".

Mr. Morgan then proposed a toast to Eaton "the best of chairman, the best of men". Overcome by the compliment, Eaton could only quote his predecessor, saying "When the heart is full it does not always run out of the mouth". He then proposed a toast to James Frederick and prior to the presentation read aloud the inscription on the watch "Presented by the Choral Society and their friends to Mr. J. F. Hill the chorus master in token of their sense of his valuable service . January 18th 1858". The purse and watch were then handed to James Frederick with the comment that should the time piece prove to be only half as accurate in performance as he was, there would be no reason to complain. The part song "Oh time is sweet when roses meet" was then sung, the music being composed by James Frederick.

Great applause erupted as the recipient rose to reply. He was not accustomed to public speaking and apologised for this, hoping it would be understood if his speech was brief. After conveying his sincere thanks to everyone for the kind manner in which the testimonial had been presented to him, he quipped that in the past had his attendance as conductor not always been punctual it was because his watch was incorrect.

CHAPTER 14
James Frederick at the Crystal Palace

After a lapse of nearly 2 years the choral society resumed their concerts in March 1858 with a performance of Haydn's "Creation". Receiving the support of an audience of 1400, it was evident the popularity of these concerts had not diminished.

On 26th May 1858 James Frederick attended the Glee Club dinner held in the club room of the Bell Hotel. On this Wednesday evening he had the company of 60 gentlemen amongst whom were Mr. R. Kerrison, Mr. H. Morgan, the secretary Mr. C. Oury and the club's conductor Horace Hill. During the winter months the Club had given 17 concerts. James Frederick's madrigal "Whilome in Fairyland" and an overture by Horace having been performed. The latter gained the warm encomiums of the club's chairman Samuel Bignold. Mr. Proops, who was receiving singing tuition from Horace, also made his debut. It was thought this young tenor, when more advanced in his studies, would become a great asset to the city's musical corps.

The cultivation of voices to the standard required by the choral society, came under the control of Mr. H. Rudd. His elementary musical tuition classes forming the necessary nursery ground for the society. In October, the "Upper" of these classes gave a concert of part songs and solos in the "best possible taste" so James Frederick could select those most suited to fill the vacancies within the choral body.

Two weeks after this selection concert, the 3rd choral concert was given. "Israel in Egypt" had been performed in July but this time a miscellaneous programme was chosen. Violinist, Herr Molique, was invited to take part. It was his first visit to Norwich. The man's appearance resembled that of a jolly English farmer in his Sunday suit rather than a distinguished musician but his playing delighted his audience. The band on this occasion however could not maintain the improvement shown during the previous 2 concerts. The choral contribution also received criticism, their choice of 2 part songs by Mendelssohn being considered unwise. These works had not been intended for such a large body of singers and this marred their beauty.

Early in the new year James Frederick with some 50 musicians travelled from Norwich to East Dereham, to assist with a concert in the Town Hall organised by Mr. Israel Lane. Lane had been a member of the Norwich Choral Society for some 40 years and had been one of the Norwich contingent at the 1857 Handel Festival. Around that time Israel left Norwich and moved to East Dereham. On finding it an "unmusical region", he aimed to cultivate a local interest in music. His concert was the first of its kind in the town. James Frederick conducted this 2 part concert in front of a full hall. Mr. Proops was one of the principal singers and Horace Hill presided at the harmonium. The city's musical events were overshadowed by the spectacular Handel Centenary Celebration Festival at the Crystal Palace in June. James Frederick, with other selected Norwich singers formed part of the 2,700 strong chorus. The festival was on an even grander scale than that of 1857 and attracted 81,260 visitors, who listened to performances of the "Messiah", "Dettingen Te Deum" and "Israel in Egypt". The festival organisers, the Sacred Harmonic Society, sent a letter of gratification to James Frederick for his very efficient and valuable service, begging his acceptance of a miniature bust of Handel and a photograph of the occasion.

Although Norwich had no spectacular musical events in 1859, the choral society under the conductorship of James Frederick, performed "Dettingen Te Deum" in March, "Elijah" in July and a miscellaneous concert in October. This 3rd concert featured an overture by Horace Hill and Pierson's part song "May Morning".

On the night of 14th July Norwich citizens witnessed a disastrous spectacle when at about 10.30pm Noble's organ factory in Pottergate caught fire. This lofty 3 story building was situated between the Militia Hospital to the west and the home of Mr. Spinks to the east. The rear of the factory premises to the east adjoined the Friends Meeting House in Upper Goat Lane. Only the front of the building was constructed of brick, the back being entirely of wood. The wooden roof was covered with asphalt to which had been applied several coatings of tar. As Mr. Spinks sat in his back room, he saw flames burst through the roof at the west end of the factory. The fire quickly spread to the whole upper story which was used as a store room and consequently full of dry timber. The Leviathan, City and Exhibition fire engines were summoned and a strong body of militia soon arrived at the scene as well as a large crowd of on-lookers. 2 water pipes were taken through the central front gateway but the heat was so intense that the fire had to be fought from the roof tops of the dwellings on the opposite side of the street. 10 sick, partly clothed men had to be evacuated from the hospital and a hole knocked through the wall to allow water pipes to reach the flames. By 1.30am the fire was under control but Noble had lost all his stock which included 3 fine organs near completion.

The cause of the fire was unknown. When workmen left the premises at 7.45pm that evening everything was safe. No fire had been lit in the factory for 3 days.

By 13th August Noble had resumed trading in part of the Bazaar in St. Andrew's Broad Street.

On the 11th and 12th October, those in pursuit of more leisurely activities spent an evening in the company of Charles Dickens in St. Andrew's Hall. Here the author read aloud extracts from his books. The man looked old for his years. His voice was not powerful but he applied a different tone for each of his character. His portrayal of little Dombey being of a whining, discontented, unlovable child.

Charles Dickens

CHAPTER 15

The Childrens' Festival

Every week from February 1860 James Frederick drilled the chorus in readiness for the September festival. By April the organ had been declared inadequate for accompaniment and a meeting was held with the corporation to decide its future. At the suggestion of the festival committee, it was agreed to add a 7 stop swell division and change the clarion to an open wood flute. The work was entrusted to Mark Noble and the cost shared between the festival committee and the corporation, the former paying £68 (4). The festival was only 2 weeks away when a fire broke out in St Andrew's Hall. A secluded door connecting the hall to the workhouse was thrown back against a gas lamp, causing the upper panel to burn through. As the heat scorched the timbers of the side galleries which were under construction, the fire was spotted by the door man who quickly dealt with the situation. The vigilance of this man saved the building from disastrous consequences.

The festival had always been preceded by a series of promenade concerts. This year the last of these concerts on the Monday evening was replaced by a performance of the "Creation". The greatly reduced entrance charge of 5/- aimed to give those of lesser means the opportunity to hear an oratorio. A "tolerable admixture of classes" filled the hall that evening. Clara Novello sang the part of Gabriel. This much loved soprano had chosen the festival to make her farewell from public life.

Tuesday brought inclement weather and a reduced attendance for the evening miscellaneous concert. The programme was exceedingly long; Mlle. Tietjens and Sig. Giuglini having been engaged at short notice. The couple, who when initially approached in November demanded extravagant fees, suddenly offered their services for favourable terms. Their additional items considerably extended the length of the concert.The first part included a song "To please and to instruct mankind" and a chorus "In Paeans loud" from the oratorio "Hypatia" by James Frederick Hill. These "pleasing compositions excited a desire" to hear more of this work. The clocks chimed midnight before the concluding overture, from Hérold's opera "Zampa" began and the work was drowned in the noise and disruption of the majority of the audience vacating the hall.

The sunshine on Wednesday morning brought 1100 people to

Tietjens

hear Handel's "Dettingen" and Spohr's "Last Judgement". The latter being performed as a tribute to the composer who had died on 22nd October 1859.

That evening Benedict returned to the orchestra to commence the second part, to find the score for the opening item, Haydn's Symphony No 5, had disappeared. A quick decision had to be made and the final work of the programme, the overture from "Der Freischütz" by Weber was hastily repositioned. This resulted in the evening's entertainment ending 15 minutes earlier than scheduled.

A new oratorio "Abraham" by Molique, received its first performance on Thursday morning, conducted by the composer. It went extremely well, the band executing their parts in a faultless manner. At the rehearsal Molique became so overjoyed by James Frederick's interpretation of the work that he embraced him planting a kiss on both cheeks, much to the amusement of the chorus.

Another first performance was given Thursday evening, this time of "Undine", a cantata composed by Benedict. The sparkling fairy like character of his music spellbound the audience into total concentration. Benedict was so impressed with the performance that he presented James Frederick with a gold pencil case.

The festival concluded Friday morning with a performance of the "Messiah". This single performance added £1055 to the festival accounts. By evening the hall had been transformed into a ballroom, decorated with evergreens and flowers. The great orchestra was crowded with spectators. The small band of 30 players included Horace, on clarionet. Although the ball had been advertised as "Fancy Dress" only 3 of the 400 attending, came as "fancies". The unwanted attention which their costumes drew proved too embarrassing and the 3 made a hasty escape by fly. The food lacked in quantity and quality. The sandwiches were dry but coffee, negus and ices were in abundance.

The festival made a profit of £918 of which £800 went to charity.

James Frederick received the sum of £32 for rehearsals, £21 for 2 promenade concerts and £30 for the festival (13).

A musical treat was in store for 6000 Sunday School children of all denominations on 24th and 25th of September in St. Andrew's Hall. The mayor, Mr. Tillett wanted the youngsters to have something to remember. Each evening 3000 children assembled outside the hall and at 6.30pm were marshalled into their seats by their teachers. The galleries had been replaced after the ball enabling the hall to be filled as for a festival concert. The evening commenced with everyone singing the hymn "Before Jehovah's awful throne" to the tune of the Old 100th. The choral society, conducted by James Frederick, then gratuitously performed a selection from the "Messiah" and the "Creation". The young listeners cheered and waved their programmes with delight. During the evening buns were distributed.

At the conclusion of the second evening concert, the mayor expressed his thanks to the choral society for the enjoyment they had given these children saying "Norwich has always been proud of its choral society, it will be more proud henceforth from our recollection of your kindness on this occasion". At 9pm the singing of the National Anthem brought the festivities to a close.

The choral society's annual tea took place in Mr. Noverre's "capacious and handsome" rooms in October. Mr. Harvard of the

Market Place provided and served a most excellent tea with dessert to the 120 members. After the cloth had been removed, Mr. Eaton spoke on behalf of the ladies of the society and presented James Frederick with a silver mounted baton and a ring, which the ladies had purchased by subscription. During the course of the evening a discussion took place on the feasibility of moving the organ and orchestra to the east end of St. Andrew's Hall. By removing a screen which hid the tower from view, the organ could be repositioned under the tower and the orchestra placed in front on a dais. It was thought this new arrangement would create space for an additional 400/500 seats.

As the end of the year approached, the citizens of Norwich experienced extreme cold. On Christmas day the temperature fell to 3 degrees Fahrenheit. At Costessey minus 7 Fahrenheit, 39 degrees below the freezing point of water, was recorded. Ice was 4 inches thick (2).

Even the severity of the weather could not deter 700 people from attending a concert in St. Andrew's Hall in January 1861, when an evening of sacred music was given by the choral society under the direction of James Frederick, for the Young Men's Christian Association. The Association had been formed 4 years previous and had 346 members.

The choral society also performed a selection of sacred music for the first of their own concerts in March. The oratorio "Judas Maccabaeus" was given in July. Sims Reeves had been engaged to sing the leading tenor part but the day before the concert a telegraphic message arrived from the tenor, who was still in Scarborough. He requested the postponement of the concert for he was unable to return to Norwich in time. The society felt at such a late hour, postponement was impossible and the services of George Perren were acquired. The work was performed admirably to a crowded hall.

With the forming of volunteer military forces over the past 2 years, military bands were everywhere and band contests, common place. In August 1861 such a contest was held in the Victoria Gardens. James Frederick was one of the 3 judges. Just a few people had gathered to listen to the 7 competing bands until the contest for the best cornet player became rather heated. The only entrant played a simple piece. Trouble brewed as Mr. Jackson, who previously had refused to enter the contest, decided to take part. A friend of Jackson's jumped on to the platform shouting at the spectators for their support. The lessee of the gardens, Mr. Ablitt, became rather concerned. He summoned the police who removed the friend. Jackson was granted permission to play, but the prize was given to the original performer.

CHAPTER 16

The Choral Society's trip to Whitlingham

1862 was to be a turning point in James Frederick's life for he suffered a stoke whilst teaching which left him paralysed. The choral society started the year with their annual meeting, held this time in the Old Library Room of St. Andrew's Hall. Here they agreed to gratuitously offer their services to the mayor for any charitable function.

When the society learned a private organiser had arranged for Jenny Lind Goldschmidt to give 2 concerts in March, it was viewed as a threat to their existence. March was traditionally the time of their first concert and the act was seen as a deliberate move to damage the society. Eaton complained bitterly and the concerts were postponed until April.

The society's first concert went ahead on 26th March 1862 with a performance of the "Messiah". Despite the inclement weather and the "great concert looming in the distance", the hall was well filled. James Frederick had brought the voices to a state of perfection for which he received great credit.

The first of Jenny Lind's concerts on 10th April featured a miscellaneous programme, opening with the first movement of Beethoven's grand trio in B$\flat$ for piano, violin and cello but the audience paid little attention to the music. Rapturous applause greeted the Swedish Nightingale as she came forward to sing "For though a cloud sometimes concealeth" from Weber's "Der Freischütz" but it revealed her voice had lost its pristine purity and clarity. The second concert on 11th was a performance of the "Creation" with Jenny taking the principal soprano part. Her husband, Otto, conducted. The ad hoc chorus had been trained by Mr. Rudd. Members of the choral society had flatly refused to take part when it came apparent they would not be under the leadership of their "clever master". They viewed it as a plan to shelve James Frederick. The choruses were, therefore, well below the standard expected from James Frederick's loyal body of singers. At short notice soloist Sims Reeves was troubled with hoarseness and withdrew. A replacement had to be found and Mr. Burton kindly consented to take his place. Only 1300 people attended. The admission charge of 1 guinea for a single ticket was considered far too high for a city under a commercial depression and the concert was branded a failure.

The annual choral society tea in 1862 took place in August at Whitlingham. 100 members and friends partook of an excellent meal and then went down to the mouth of the cave to sing glees, their voices awakening the "echoes of this romantic locality". The company returned to the House* at about 7.30pm. Loyal and patriotic toasts were proposed and received with enthusiasm and a pleasant memorable evening was had by everyone present.

The second concert in the society's calendar, a performance of Costa's "Eli" was postponed until October as a large number of the society's subscribers were out of the city for the International Exhibition which had opened in London during May.

The following month a miscellaneous concert was given. The services of Mr. Haigh and Sig. Ciampi (The primo buffo of the Royal Italian Opera in Covent Garden) had been engaged. The concert commenced with Romberg's overture in D. Mr. Haigh nervously sang a rather poor song "A Young and Artless Maiden" by Howard Glover and Mr. Thouless, an organ student of Mr. Harcourt, played most efficiently a Mendelssohn prelude and Bach's pedal fugue in G. A selection from Pierson's "To Arms" was effectively sung with "spirit and martial fire" by the chorus and the concert was brought to a close with the singing of the National Anthem.

Both concerts were conducted by James Frederick, who concluded the year by conducting a Norwich Vocal Society concert in the Noverre Room. It was the third such occasion. Henry Smart's part song "The Shepherd's Farewell" was one of the items performed and the numerous attendance warmly appreciated the efforts of all concerned.

In the new year James Frederick announced his resumption to teaching. Classes were to begin in St. Andrew's Hall on Wednesday 21st January 1863 for treble voices commencing at 8 o'clock, followed by other voices at 9 o'clock. The next day private lessons were to be given at his home, 4 St Giles Terrace; teaching ladies at 8 o'clock and gentlemen at 9 o'clock.

* Whitlingham White House Tavern was a popular pleasure locality. The tavern operated a ferry across the river to Thorpe St. Andrew. (12). By 1864 the tavern had been demolished for the building of a Lodge for the Crown Point Estate Mansion. (12).

CHAPTER 17

Alterations to St. Andrew's Hall

Until the festival in September, concerts in 1863 were severely restricted, owing to the restoration of St. Andrew's Hall. However James Frederick did conduct the Norwich Vocal Society's 4th concert in the Noverre Room during April. This programme of duets, glees, songs and madrigals delighted the listeners to such an extent that several encores were given.

By May restoration work on the hall was in full progress. A new south porch was under construction and the plastered, white washed surface of the south wall was being refaced with flints. Extensive repairs were also being carried out to the roof, the structure having been declared to be like elastic, had some of the existing lead, after recasting, relaid. Inside the hall, 4 retiring rooms were near completion. Numerous coatings of paint had been stripped from the pillars and the pillar bases, the latter having now been reinstated after being cut away at some point, to maximise floor space.

The east wall, where Nelson's portrait hung, had been removed, throwing open the tower and revealing evidence of a former arch. A grand new arch 30 ft wide had yet to be constructed and the organ was still awaiting its relocated beneath the tower.

By the end of the month work had begun on rebuilding the west wall. It proved to be a difficult task; it overhung the pathway in Bridge St. by 1 foot and arched buttresses were put in place to allow pedestrians to pass beneath. Throughout the restoration, the builder J. W. Lacey of Surrey St. (11) and mason Mr. Stanley ensured the safety of their workmen by encasing St. Andrew's Hall in "sufficient" scaffolding.

The intention of the architect, Mr. Barry, was to return the hall to a building the city and county could view with pride and admiration. Not everyone agreed with this sentiment and several letters appeared in the press expressing disapproval. The main target, the new south porch, provoked letters from readers signing themselves "Black Friar" and "Anti South Porch".

In July, workmen digging a trench across the old preaching yard for the new gas supply, uncovered a number of skeletons just below the surface. The area had been used as a burial ground in 1579; at a time when the plague was haunting the citizens of Norwich. Workmen laboured tirelessly to complete the hall in readiness for the festival. For 5 weeks rooms in the Lecture Hall in St. Andrew's St. were hired from Mr. Jarrold for the sale of tickets.

To celebrate the hall's completion, the mayor held a "Déjeuner" on 12th August. James Frederick was one of the 200 invited guests. He sat at one of the 2 long tables which stretched down the length of the nave. Dignitaries were seated at a table across the east end. An excellent bill of fare was spread before them with pineapples, peaches, apricots and grapes forming the dessert. The wines, claret and port were supplied by Norgate & Sons. But the meal was spoilt by the ineffective waiting service. With guests restricted to the food within arms reach few could find sufficient palatable fare to make a meal. The following day the hall seated 200 workmen who were given a cold dinner with a supply of beer. The Carrow Works band entertained both during and after the meal.

The festival commenced on the evening of Monday 14th September with a selection from "Judas Maccabaeus". The newly decorated hall was illuminated by 500 gas jets. The brilliance of the white walls and pillars dazzled the audience who found the bright glare most trying on the eyes. The roof panels, painted aqua marine, were studded with golden stars. The spandrels coloured with blue, brown, red and white. To the majority, the hall looked gaudy and totally out of keeping with the original architecture.

On hearing the first strains of the National Anthem, the audience of 1300 rose to their feet. The sound from the organ in its recess under the tower demonstrated it had lost a lot of its power in the void which surrounded it, instead of being projected, as expected, through the arch like the mouth of a trumpet. James Frederick had prepared the festival chorus of 77 sopranos, 23 contraltos, 38 altos, 64 tenors and 80 basses. They were divided into 3 sections. One in each aisle and the third in front of the arch. This new location was most pleasing for their voices no longer recoiled as they previously had done.

By the ended of the concert, at 11.30pm, the heat within the hall had become excessive. The new south porch was branded unsafe for ladies as the violent contrasts in temperature experienced therein was considered bad for their health.

On Tuesday evening only 69 people occupied the patrons gallery in its new location at the west end. Beethoven's "Pastorale" symphony opened the first part of the programme. Mr. Cusins conducted his "Serenata". Sims Reeves sang "The Message" by

Blumenthal and it was 10.30pm before the second part began, opening with Weber's overture from "Oberon". A selection from Gounod's "Faust" was sung for the first time and as the hands of the clock moved together, Bishop's song "Sleep Gentle Lady" was appropriately sung. By the time the final work, the overture from Mozart's "Il Flauto Magico" had been completed, the hall was virtually empty.

Wednesday morning's concert also had a low attendance for new works from untried composers seldom drew large crowds. Silas conducted his oratorio "Joash", his conducting skills showing he was not accustomed to the baton. The libretto, compiled by George Lindley was said to be both unlyrical and undignified but the audience were well pleased with the performance and could not be kept within the confines of no applause. Mr. A. H. Thouless' new work "Ave Maria" also received high praise. This young, Norwich born, musician was a pupil of Mr. Harcourt and held the post of assistant organist both at St. Peter Mancroft and the festival. The melody was of a most agreeable nature giving great pleasure and the work was thought worthy of future performances. The programme concluded with the "Hallelujah" from Beethoven's "Mount of Olives".

Spohr's symphony in D opened the miscellaneous concert in the evening. A selection from Mozart's operas, a quartet from Flotow's "Martha" and the trio "I Naviganti" by Randegger were performed before the concert ended with the overture from Auber's opera "Fra Diavolo".

On Thursday morning the choruses from "Elijah" were excellently sung. Julius Benedict was so impressed he exclaimed to James Frederick that such singing could not be bettered anywhere in the world. This popular concert drew an attendance of 1423.

The final miscellaneous concert on Thursday evening included Haydn's "Surprise" symphony, "Coeur De Lion" by Benedict, the overture to G. A. Macfarren's "Don Quixote" and concluded with Weber's "Invitation a la Valse".

A performance of the "Messiah" on Friday brought the festival to a close. No time was wasted in sending a "certificate" to Mr. Barry conveying to him the success of the new orchestra. One of the signatories was James Frederick.

The galleries were still being removed as people began to arrive for the ball. The wearing of fancy dress had been discontinued and gentlemen were encouraged to wear their military uniforms. Mirrors lined the walls and fuchsias graced the window sills. James Frederick accompanied Miss Hill and at 10.00pm the dancing of quadrilles, lancers, galops and valses commenced to the music of Mr. Howlett's band. 400 people paid to gaze at the spectacle from the orchestra adding £50 to the receipts.

The attendance at the festival totalled 8246, a figure only surpassed in 1824 and 1827.

Throughout the week an engraved copy of a painting by Copley, "The Fall of Major Pearson in Jersey in 1780", had been exhibited in the choral society's waiting room in St. Andrew's Hall together with a list of subscribers. This picture of Hugo Pierson's ancestor was presented to the composer as a token of their admiration of his "genius".

CHAPTER 18

Entertaining at the Y.M.C.A.

The new year again brought severe weather, providing excellent ice for skating. A temperature of 14 degrees Fahrenheit was recorded at Earlham. On 7th January 1864 the festival guarantors held their general meeting at the Shirehall. A vote of thanks was given to James Frederick for his efficient service throughout the festival.

The previous evening Mr. Lambert Wilkes had lectured in the Free Library on the subject of the "Decimal System of Coinage and Accounts". Wilkes put forward the advantages of having just one divisor of 10, instead of those used of 4,12, and 20. He claimed the system, if universally adopted, could reduce the time spent in the counting house by one fourth. His radical ideas brought forth frequent applause.

The ladies and gentlemen of the choral society gathered for tea at the Bell Hotel on the evening of Tuesday 12th January 1864. Mr. Francis Gostling and his family were invited as special guests. Gostling had been assistant secretary of the choral society for the past 7 years and had stepped down from office. A presentation of a handsome piano was made to him by Mr. Eaton in appreciation of his past service. The instrument costing 35 guineas had been purchased from Messrs. Howlett's. Following tea, toasts and glees filled the remainder of the evening, one toast being to their leader Mr. James Frederick Hill.

Exactly a week later James Frederick attended the annual social tea of the Young Men's Christian Association held in St. Andrew's Hall. During the evening the Association's private band and a choir under the direction of James Frederick performed a selection of light sacred and secular music.

The Y.M.C.A.'s February meeting also had the services of James Frederick. On this occasion he directed a choir of 50 voices, giving musical illustrations to a lecture on psalmody presented by the Reverend Henry Allon of Islington. The reverend gentleman complimented the choir saying their fine singing excelled that of the Harmonic Society of Exeter Hall.

The choral society's first concert took place in March. Of late these thrice yearly concerts had lacked support. The society had generously given money to charity and also established a fund for distressed society members and their families. This, it was thought, had created the impression of a wealthy existence. Receipts diminished, outlay augmented and the society found themselves fighting a financial battle. The public were reminded of the importance of these concerts, not only did they keep the chorus in a state of efficiency for the festival but also relieved the festival fund of financially supporting a chorus during the interim years. The public took heed and although the sheriff's dinner fell on the same evening, St. Andrew's Hall was well filled. The chosen programme, Mendelssohn's "St Paul", was however unwise. The work was described as being "unbearably heavy" and "overburdened with long recitatives" which "sorely tried the patience of the audience". Although the choruses went reasonably well, they were not perfect. There was no special feature of beauty or grandness. Master Mann, of the cathedral, sang the air "But the Lord is Mindful" most successfully but despite his admirable performance there was still an expressed desire that "St. Paul" should not be repeated.

James Frederick gave a concert on the evening of Thursday 9th June 1864 in the Noverre Room where he conducted a programme of miscellaneous pieces by Meyerbeer, Auber, Bishop, Gounod, Benedict's "Old May Day" , his own arrangements of the quintett "Sacred Peace" from Storace's little opera "No Song, No Supper" and the quartet and chorus from "Martha" by Flotow. The latter concluded the entertainment. Mr. Thouless accompanied on the piano throughout the concert. Congratulations were conferred upon James Frederick for producing such an enjoyable evening with comparatively slender resources.

Earlier that day Mr. Roger Kerrison was buried at Kirstead, having died at his Tombland home on 2nd of June 1864. His familiar face and light hearted gossip would be greatly missed within the festival circle where, of late, he had held the position of honorary secretary.

The second choral society concert did not take place until 21st October. Grisi and Mario had been engaged as principal soloists. This miscellaneous concert had all the makings of being the society's most attractive concert for some time. Tickets sales were high. On the day of the concert however the public were informed that the couple would not be performing. One of their daughters had become dangerously ill. The information had been received so late that postponement was impossible and the services of Miss Marion Moss and Wilbye Cooper were hastily secured. They were inefficient substitutes for the great singers but the large audience bore their disappointment with good humour. Miss Moss, who was making her debut under these trying circumstances, was warmly encouraged with hearty applause, but although her voice showed some good qualities she had much to learn. Mde Sainton Dolby who had been engaged as a supporting artist, suddenly found herself promoted to principal performer. She nobly acquitted herself but her voice showed signs of deterioration. However she sang Henry Smart's ballad "The Lady of the Sea" faultlessly, causing an encore to be demanded. The concert concluded with the chorus "Victoria Our Queen" by Rossini. Although well performed it received little attention from the audience as they prepared for their departure. 1400 people had been squeezed into the Hall. The space allotted to each person did not cater for the crinoline, resulting in much discomfort. This contributed greatly to the concert, which had started out with such good prospects, being judged as the least enjoyable given by the society.

The third choral society concert followed a month later with performances of "Undine" and Handel's "Alexander's Feast". The hall again was well filled. Benedict conducted his own work which was warmly applauded throughout and he was twice recalled at its conclusion. The "Feast" was conducted by James Frederick, it too giving great satisfaction.

In the new year of 1865 James Frederick again assisted with the entertainment at the Y.M.C.A. annual tea in St. Andrew's Hall. The interior of the hall had been tastefully decorated with evergreens, flowers and banners. The president, J. J. Colman, addressed the gathering, informing them of an increase in membership to 420. A choir under the conductorship of James Frederick then sang appropriate pieces.

A benefit concert for Mr. A.H. Thouless was given on 17th February. Thouless was leaving Norwich to study at the Royal Academy. His remarkable proficiency as an organist and pianist had been a great asset to the city. Two of his own compositions appeared on the programme, a scena "Hohenlinden", sung by Mr. Poole and an overture written especially for the occasion. The former was not performed as Mr. Poole was injured on his journey to Norwich. Whilst sitting in a railway carriage at Wymondham station he was suddenly thrown from his seat when an additional carriage was forcefully added to the train. The internal injuries he sustained prevented him from singing.

Arthur Sullivan

Arthur Sullivan

1858

James Frederick conducted the choral society's first concert of 1865, "The Creation", on 30th March. Instrumentalist from Great Yarmouth, Kings Lynn and London assisted the band. The numerous attendance and rapturous applause deemed the concert a success.

5 weeks later Mme. Grisi returned to the city to take part in a concert promoted by Charles Hall in aid of the Jenny Lind Infirmary. Arthur Sullivan came to conduct. Grisi's voice revealed it had lost most of its purity and freshness through the inroads of Time but its power still astonished her listeners as she sang "Qui la Voce" from Bellini's "I Puritani", "Home Sweet Home" and "The Minstrel Boy". Keen to make amends for her previous "unfortunate default" with the choral society, she readily consented to numerous calls for encores. Her audience however was small and had it not been for Mr. Gedge inviting the Volunteers and their wives, many of the benches would have remained empty. The concert yielded little profit for the cause but Mr. Hall liberally presented £40 to the Infirmary.

The choral society over the past year had incurred heavy losses. Their financial situation had become severe and they were forced to abandon any thoughts of further public concerts in 1865. But in order to keep themselves in readiness for the next festival, rehearsals were opened to the public once a month at a small charge. The first took place on Monday 18th September 1865 under the patronage of the mayor, Mr. Tuck. A comfortably filled St. Andrew's Hall listened to a rehearsal of "Judas Maccabaeus". Over the following months these public rehearsals featured Perry's "Death of Abel", "The Creation", the "Mount of Olives", "Alexander's Feast" and "Elijah" ending on 18th December with a rehearsal of the "Messiah". All were conducted by James Frederick, whose busy year concluded by conducting a Norwich Vocal Society concert in Mr. Noverre's room.

CHAPTER 19

The visit of the Prince of Wales in 1866

Many of the choral society's members had been singing for upwards of 40 years. Now old, their voices had grown tired. The time had come to reconstruct the chorus in readiness for the next festival. Anyone with a desire to sing was invited to be examined for competency by James Frederick. Several fresh young voices were among the 247 selected. All pledged to be diligent and attend rehearsals regularly. Having conducted Jackson's Te Deum and Haydn's "O be Joyful" at the annual Y. M. C. A. social tea in January, James Frederick turned his attentions to drilling the new festival chorus.

The Prince and Princess of Wales expressed a desire to attend the festival and so to comply with their wishes the event was delayed until late October, the first concert being on the evening of Monday 29th. Every exertion was made to make the festival worthy of such honoured guests but holding it so late in the year caused anxieties. The top Italian soloists could not be engaged for they had returned to the continent having finished their tour of England. Consequently some of the soloist came from Mr. Mapleson's* "cage of singing birds". These singers held little attraction, being considered below the standard of those usually engaged. There was also doubt whether people would venture out in the darker evenings.

These concerns soon dissipated as the hall filled to capacity to hear G. Macfarren's version of "Israel in Egypt", its popularity causing many to be turned away at the door. The work had only just commenced when Benedict turned to the audience and in a near inaudible voice announced that a message had been received stating Mr. Sims Reeves was too ill to perform. The news was mocked in disbelief. Hissing reverberated around the hall but Mr. Cummings obligingly agreed to take on Sims Reeves part as well as his own, singing both most sensibly and respectably.

Sims Reeves was absent on Tuesday evening. Cummings again offered his services. His singing of Fèlicien David's serenade "Oh ma Maitresse" being so full of eloquence, expression and sentiment, it deservedly won an encore.

The concert had the honoured presence of the Duke of Edinburgh whose entrance during the performance of Beethoven's Septet was so unobtrusive, few noticed his arrival. The Duke had

William Cummings

Fèlicien David

journeyed from Sandringham earlier in the evening.

At the commencement of the second part, Arthur Sullivan took the baton to conduct his "In Memoriam" which had been composed expressly for the festival. The work was thought to be in memory of his father who had died a few months earlier. Although faultlessly performed it was considered far too mournful for a miscellaneous evening concert.

The city awoke Wednesday morning to the sound of church bells which rang out from the early hours to mark the visit of the Prince and Princess of Wales. By breakfast the city streets were lined with people eagerly awaiting the arrival of the Royal party. Strong barriers had been put in place along the route from St. Giles to the Guildhall to hold back the crowds. A stand had been erected in St Giles, at the expense of J. J. Colman, for children over 9 years of age from the Carrow and St. Giles schools. Public stands had been erected in the gaol gardens and in front of many shops. All were speedily occupied. Banners and bunting decorated the streets and flags flew from the church steeples.

Triumphal Arch
St. Giles Gate 1866

Reproduced by kind permission of the Norfolk Record Office

By 11 o'clock the mayor, Mr. Nichols, and civic dignitaries had assembled at the city boundary, at St. Giles' Gate, the mayor being conveyed in a very handsome carriage and four loaned for the day by R. J. H. Harvey. At 10 minutes past eleven the volunteer artillery in Chapelfield fired a Royal salute. Somehow they had been misinformed as 25 minutes elapsed before the Royal party came into view escorted by the Norwich Light Horse.

In the first carriage was the Prince and Princess of Wales, the Queen of Denmark and the Earl of Leicester. In the second, their hosts Lord and Lady Stafford. At St. Giles' Gate the party halted to greet the mayor and his entourage who then formed part of the procession. As they passed, the children sang "God Bless the Prince of Wales". Loud cheers accompanied the procession all the way to the Guildhall, with the bells of St. Peter Mancroft ringing forth to herald their arrival. The reception in the council chambers took longer than anticipated.

In St. Andrew's Hall, the concert began without them but little notice was taken of the music as the audience watched and listened for the Royal party. During the first performance of Costa's "Naaman", the party arrived having travelled via Exchange St., Post Office St. and St. Andrew's St., entering the hall by the cloisters on the north side. The commotion both outside and inside halted the performance. The audience rose to welcome them and when the excitement had finally subsided, the performance continued. Unfortunately for Costa no encores were given, nobody would signal before their honoured guests. Sims Reeves sang magnificently, showing no signs of malaise. After the performance Costa was summoned to the private Royal apartments, which had been elaborately furnished by Messrs. Trevor and Page, where he was highly complemented on his composition.

The Royal procession left St. Andrew's Hall at half past two for Chapelfield, going by way of Prince's St., Tombland, King St., London St., the Market Place, Brigg St., Rampant Horse St. and St. Stephen's St. At Chapelfield the Prince planted trees in the recently laid out formal gardens before opening the new drill shed.

In the evening Sims Reeves was again indisposed for which no apology was made. The miscellaneous programme commenced with Mendelssohn's "A Midsummer Night's Dream" and concluded with the March from Molique's "Abraham" instead of the advertised "Triumphal March" from Meyerbeer's "L'Africaine"

During the evening works by Nicolai, Rossini, Weber and Gounod were performed. The many encores greatly extended the concert, it being a quarter past eleven before the music finally concluded.

On Thursday morning a well filled hall listened to Handel's Passion music. It was the first time the work had been performed in England. Although composed in 1704, it had only been published a few years earlier. The "Legend of St. Cecilia" by Benedict with words by Henry F. Chorley, followed. This cantata had been composed especially for the festival. The lengthy morning programme concluded with 2 parts of Haydn's "Creation".

Outside the streets thronged with people hoping to catch another glimpse of the Prince and Princess of Wales as they travelled from Cossey Hall and through the city to Thorpe Station. A special train had been arranged for half past twelve to convey the Royal couple to Dereham and then on to Wolferton.

Thursday evening's miscellaneous concert was again attended by the Duke of Edinburgh. The programme opened with Beethoven's Symphony No 8 in F. and concluded with the "Hunting Chorus" from Haydn's "The Seasons".

Handel's "Messiah" on Friday morning filled the hall to the utmost, £1052-12s-6d being raised from this concert alone. Just 2 hours after its conclusion the hall had been stripped of its galleries and a handsome baronial staircase constructed on either side of the orchestra. By the evening coats of arms, exotic plants and orange trees decorated the interior. Over the west door the Prince of Wales plumes was surrounded by a very large reflective glass hung with crimson and white drapery.

Instead of the usual refreshments of negus and ices, 550 people consumed a sumptuous supper provided and served by Mr Snelling of Rampant Horse St.

Shortly after 10 o'clock the dancing commenced to the music of Mr. Walter Howlett's band positioned on a specially constructed orchestra to the south side of the hall. The company twirling the night away till half past four in the morning.

Earlier that evening 20,000 to 30,000 people had streamed from the alleys and yards, through the thoroughfares to Castle Hill to watch a spectacular firework display. At 7 o'clock the grey night sky became illuminated by magnesium lights burning from the tops of church steeples. When they died away two fire balloons ascended into the night sky, leaving a trail of fire behind them as they sailed towards Thorpe. At the top of the hill near Golden Ball St., Mr. Coe and Mr. Baxter assembled their 2 hour pyrotechnical show on a large stage. Alternately they discharged rockets, bombs and Chinese lights. Their magnificent creations included revolving globes, coats of arms and mottoes. Midway through the display, magnesium lights burned from the 4 corners of the castle keep.

At 11 o'clock an immense fire balloon with fireworks attached floated up above the city exploding at a great height. The whole event went off without a single accident or disturbance.

The week had been highly successful. After James Mottram had audited the festival accounts a profit of £971 was declared

James Frederick received a letter from Michael Costa conveying his warmest thanks for the zeal, precision and care he had taken with "Naaman". "To you sir I am also indebted for the pains you take in drilling them and permit me to congratulate you for the pleasure you must feel in presiding over such a magnificent body of fresh voices and good musicians. Believe me yours very truly M. Costa".

* Mr. J. H. Mapleson was lessee of Her Majesty's Theatre in London.

CHAPTER 20

Antonio James Oury

The Norwich Choral Society tried hard to revive their subscription concerts in 1867. The first concert was planned for Lent assize week, provided a sufficient number of subscribers came forward. In the past the choral society had met with severe criticism in the way they managed their affairs, but the minor alterations they now put in place did little to win back subscribers. Consequently the concert did not materialise.

The festival committee became increasingly concerned. Although the choral society was making every effort to resuscitate their body, steps had to be taken to secure the future of the festival.

The celebrated violinist, M. Antonio James Oury*, was therefore asked by the festival committee to settle in Norwich so that he could prepare a band and chorus in readiness for the festival. This he was willing to do for a fee of £120 per year. The violinist had assisted with other grand musical festival in England and was no stranger to Norwich having first appeared in a "matinee musicale" on 16th July 1839 at the home of Mde. Oury Crook in Chapel Field. (2)

At a general meeting of the festival committee held in April 1867 at Dr. Copeman*'s residence, it was proposed that a chorus and band, known as the Festival Chorus and Band be formed and kept under a committee of Dr. Buck, Dr. Copeman, the Rev. Henry Symonds, J. B. Morgan, T. D. Eaton and W. Howlett. Oury was officially engaged for the aforementioned sum and had the support of a chorus master and organist who received £20 and £15 respectively. The public were invited to become subscribers. Every guinea subscribed being rewarded with 2 free tickets to each concert in the series.

Although Norwich lacked choral concerts in 1867 it still had high class musical entertainment. On 12th February the celebrated violinist Joseph Joachim gave a concert in the Noverre Room accompanied by Charles Hallé, piano; Piatti, violoncello; Zerbini, viola; and Herr L. Ries second violin. Their playing of works by Haydn, Beethoven and Mendelssohn brought forth rapturous applause at the conclusion of every movement.

The first Festival Choral Society concert took place in October 1867. This miscellaneous concert was hastily arranged to take advantage of the soloists visiting the area at the time. Mde.

Joseph Joachim

Lemmens Sherrington (soprano), Miss Lucy Franklein (contralto), Mr. Nelson Varley (tenor) and Sig Ronchetti (bass) agreed to take part. Oury played a violin concerto with perfect intonation. Mde. Lemmens Sherrington sang "Home Sweet Home". Nelson Varley sang "Sound the Alarm" from "Judas Maccabaeus" and "If with all your Hearts" from "Elijah"; his clear articulation and expressive power making him a possible successor to Sims Reeves, provided he received the correct tuition. The choruses however, although sung well, were so loud they annihilated the band. A mediocre audience sat through the concert in extreme discomfort. The excessive heat and an oppressive atmosphere causing many to complain. Prior to the restoration, St. Andrew's Hall had ventilators attached to the roof but these were removed when timber cladding was fixed beneath the lead. The numerous gas lights now helped to consume a limited supply of oxygen.

"Home Sweet Home"

A second festival choral concert soon followed on 12th December. "Judas Maccabaeus" with Perry's accompaniment was performed. Lucy Franklein, Mde. Cherer, Leigh Wilson and R. Farquharson being the soloists, each receiving the sum of 10 guineas (14). Unfortunately Leigh Wilson was suffering with a cold and apologised for his poor performance.

In the new year Mr. Mapleson brought his principal artists to Norwich who staged a grand operatic concert in St. Andrew's Hall on February 18th 1868. 9 encores were successfully demanded by the large audience. Her Majesty's Theatre had been consumed by fire a few months previous, so the pecuniary receipts from the concert went to Mapleson to help compensate for this disaster.

At the time of Mapleson's concert Norwich people were incensed by the actions of the City Committee. The body had acceded to the wishes of the British Association*, recommending to the full council that the Guildhall clock be changed from "Norwich Time" to Greenwich Time. Citizens thought the idea quite ludicrous. They were well aware of the correct time and considered it an insult to their intelligence to have to observe the time at Greenwich. They could see no advantage at all in having their clocks 5.2 minutes behind the actual time. (The railways used Greenwich time for their train schedules but this was popularly referred to as "Railway Time"). It was even mockingly suggested that the gentlemen who wanted to control the sun should come to the coast and command the tides to ebb and flow with the Thames.

On 1st March 1868 the clock in Mr. Dixon's shop window in London Street changed its face to Greenwich Time and Norwich Time was lost.

Later that month the festival chorus gave its 3rd concert, a performance of the "Messiah". This ever popular oratorio attracted a large crowd. Capt. A. H. Braham of the 15th Hussars, son of the great English tenor, sang with excellent taste bringing forth frequent applause, the no clapping rule being totally disregarded. Master Albert Livock of the cathedral choir sang the contralto part; acquitting himself most admirably. Mr. Harcourt played the organ, Mr. Oury conducted the band and James Frederick conducted the chorus.

The Vocal Society's 14th concert was held in the Noverre Room in May. The sultry state of the weather reduced the attendance. Theodore Hill, James Frederick's son was one of the performers in a programme which featured the folk songs "Sumer is icumen in" and "It was a lover and his lass". Both songs having been arranged by James Frederick who also had modernised the words of the former. These pieces were "nicely" given and received hearty applause. A serenade "Good Night" composed by James Frederick, his quintet "Sacred Peace" and a quartet "Morning Song" by Horace Hill were also heard.

Rehearsals started in July for a second series of festival choral concerts. The slow intake of subscriptions prompted the following notice to be inserted in the press on 8th August 1868:-

"We the undersigned appointed by the General Committee to keep a chorus and band in preparation for the next Festival feel it necessary to appeal to the lovers of music and the promotion of the Triennial Festival for subscriptions to the Choral Society. We hope this appeal to the musical public will meet with a ready and speedy response so that we may at once proceed with our templated arrangements. signed Z. Buck, mus. doc.; E Symonds, Precentor; J. B. Morgan, T. D. Eaton, W. Howlett and E. Copeman M.D. Chairman".

It brought results. The first concert on 15th October 1868 drew a crowd of 1200. Part 1 of the concert comprised of a selection of pieces from Handel's "Deborah", Mendelssohn's "Elijah", and Pierson's "Jerusalem". The miscellaneous second part commenced with Haydn's "Military" symphony. The terzetto from "Elijah" was sung most beautifully by Livock, Grousse and Butler of the cathedral choir, their clear articulation and purity of tone delighting those present. Mr. Wilbye Cooper was billed to sing a Recit and Air "Dreams" of his own composition but the gentleman was too ill to leave his home, the audience being informed of his absence by way of a printed announcement. Mr. H. J. Minns filled the ensuing space by singing Berger's "Geraldine", receiving deserved applause. The concluding work was Bishop's "Now Tramp". The work was capitally performed but could not be heard above the noise of company departing the hall. The evening had shown how the band had responded well to their new master, having much improved. The chorus, as expected, was excellent.

The second concert of the series was given on 22nd December. "Alexander's Feast" occupied the first part. This was not a wise choice as although rehearsals had gone well, it went most unsatisfactorily. The audience appeared some what relieved when the second part commenced with Haydn's "Surprise", the band being far more at ease with this work. At half past eleven the evening concluded with Pierson's "To Arms".

* Antonio James Oury was born in 1800 in London. His father had taken part in Bonaparte's early campaigns and was captured by the British. Young Oury received his early tuition from his father and George Macfarren. In 1812 he became a pupil of Mori and Kiesewetter and then went to Paris to studied with Kreutzer. He married pianist Mlle Belleville in 1831 and together they toured Europe giving concerts. After settling in Norwich in 1868 he moved to East Dereham where he resided with Arthur Mori until his death on 25th July 1883(2). His internment on East Dereham cemetery was witnessed by several professional gentlemen from Norwich. The grave Plot 3, 31AA is marked by a weathered arched head stone engraved with a small cross and the inscription "In Memory of Antonio James Oury F.R.A.M. , violinist, who died 25th July 1883 aged 83 years . R.I.P".

* Dr. Copeman . A prominent Norwich physician. Born on 26th December 1809 at Great Witchingham, son of Edward Breese Copeman, merchant. Educated at Trunch Grammar School. Died from heart disease at his home in the Upper Close on 25th February 1880. (2)

* The British Association of the Advancement of Science. In August 1868 the Association held their 38th Annual Meeting in Norwich; most of the lectures taking place in the new drill hall.

CHAPTER 21

The Festival Fails

The 1st January 1869 brought with it the introduction of dog licensing, at a cost of 5/- per year for each dog over 6 months old, a penalty of £5 being imposed on offenders. Another festival choral concert was given on 23rd February under the direction of James Frederick. This miscellaneous concert commenced with the overture from Mozart's "La Clemenza di Tito". The pianist, Frederick Boscovitz had brought along 3 of his own compositions "Rose et Papillon", "Chant du Soir" and "Fantasia on the Grand Duchess" but instead of his studies he played airs from "Il Trovatore" and "Home Sweet Home". The latter being played mostly entirely with the left hand. The singing of Mde. Lemmens Sherrington gave much delight, every piece receiving an encore. Nelson Varley sang remarkable well. The band was excellent and Pierson's "Now the Bright Morning Star" was sung with full force by the chorus evoking much excitement.

Preparations for the festival occupied the coming months. Liszt was invited to take part but he declined. The services of Tietjens, Patey, Cherer, Trebelli, Bettini, Rigby, Cummings, Santley and Foli were engaged. Ilma de Murska was granted permission to appear by the authorities of Baden Baden.

In order to accommodate some of the vocalists the festival was brought forward, to begin on 30th August. Many of the principal families of the city and county were still either grouse shooting in Scotland or on continental tours. In the Shirehall a Royal Commission inquiry was taking place into the alleged corrupt practices during the recent parliamentary election. The harvest was late and there were the added distractions of a flower show in the Corn Hall and a fine arts exhibition in the Lecture Hall. Subsequently the demand for tickets was low.

The audience still greeted Julius Benedict with hearty applause as he took up his place to conduct the Monday evening concert. He now had local family ties. Since the last festival his daughter had married a Norwich man. The patrons occupied the stalls in front of the orchestra and a refreshment buffet was situated under the west gallery managed by Mr. Snelling. The evening commenced with the singing of the National Anthem. Several members of the Hill family were in the chorus performing Mendelssohn's "Hymn of Praise" and Handel's "Acis and

Galatea". It was Vernon Rigby's first festival appearance, his fine tenor voice making a favourable impression. Time quickly passed and it was half past eleven before the concert concluded.

The miscellaneous programme Tuesday evening opened with Mendelssohn's "Reformation" symphony. The work had only been discovered since his death. Ilma de Murska made her debut by singing "The Shadow Song" from "Dinorah" by Meyerbeer. Her fresh clear soprano voice had a distinct individuality which captivated the audience. But to the audience's disappointment the Hungarian airs she was expected to sing were replaced by "Qui la voce" from Bellini's "I Puritani". A misunderstanding in communications had occurred for which Benedict apologised. The penultimate item, Emile Durand's "Comme a Vingt Ans" was sung by Mde Trebelli against the bustle of departing company eager to leave the hall before the final item. Wagner's March from "Tannhäuser" brought the concert to a close. It was the first time his music had been included in the festival.

The concert on Wednesday morning attracted fewer people. A selection from Pierson's new 3 part oratorio, "Hezekiah" and Spohr's "Fall of Babylon" were being performed. After Harcourt had played the overture of the former work Pierson took over at the organ. This controversial composer's work was well received and he bowed several times before vacating the orchestra. A certain section of society still verbally attacked this man branding him a "distinguished failure".

The first part of Wednesday evening's concert was devoted to Mozart. The only instrumental piece being his K239 serenata. This work for solo strings, string orchestra and timpani was still unpublished, the score being in the possession of Randegger who obligingly loaned it to the festival committee. It created a sensation among the musicians present. The light and elegant quality of the music bewitched the audience. Mr. Cumming's admirable rendition of David's "O Ma Maitresse" accompanied on the harp by Mr. Lockwood won an encore and this delightful concert was brought to a close with the overture to Auber's "Zanetta".

Thursday morning's programme of sacred music commenced with Horace Hill's cantata "Song of Praise". The work had previously been performed on 2nd December 1868 in the Noverre Room. It had since been revised. Lord Suffield and Lord Stafford were among those present to hear this talented composition in its new form. The cantata was followed by Rossini's "Messe Solennelle". Most of the audience impulsively rose for the Credo, but once standing they were unsure when to sit and many remained standing for the rest of this perfectly executed performance. There was no applause, the "no clapping" rule being totally observed. The Mass, written in 1863, had only recently been published, the Norwich performing rights being obtained from Messrs. Guy and Mapleson for a charge of £80. Handel's "Dettingen" concluded the concert.

Ilma de Murska caused a sensation on Thursday evening proving she could effortlessly soar to E in alt. Everything she sang was willingly repeated. "The Forging of the Anchor" by Benedict was also sung twice by Santley but this song with its anvil accompaniment was considered rather unsuitable for such a high class concert.

On Friday morning the "Messiah" again drew the highest attendance, with over 1500 listeners but the overall attendance was 1300 fewer than in 1866. The festival made a loss of £3-17s-4d.

No money could be given to charities so 2 Grand Miscellaneous Concerts, conducted by Julius Benedict, were arranged for 25th and 26th of November. St Andrew's Hall thronged with the elite of the city and county who paid the admission of 10/6d or 5/-. One of the 5 soloists engaged was the 23 year old Swedish singer, Mlle Christine Nilsson. Although she had appeared in London she was a stranger to Norwich.

It was hoped to raise £200 for charity but the high fees demanded by the soloists prevented this target being reached. The organisers Messrs. Gilman and Howlett generously made up the shortfall to enable £70 to be given to the Norfolk and Norwich Hospital and the Jenny Lind Hospital with a further £60 being donated to the Norwich Dispensary.

The Jenny Lind Hospital received a further £50 in December when James Frederick conducted the Norwich Choral Society in a performance of the "Messiah". Despite unfortunate weather the concert was well attended and considered a success.

At the time accusations were being made as to who was to blame for the failings of the last festival. A call was made to bar amateurs from the band for they spoiled the effect of any performance, acting as a "drag chain" upon the London professionals. The rift deepened. James Frederick and the Norwich Choral Society tried to put on a performance of the "Creation" on 29th March 1870 to raise money for alterations to the Norfolk and Norwich Hospital. Their concert was blighted by a suggestion that they were deliberately trying to mislead the public as the money required for the work had already been raised.

The concert went ahead. The audience in St. Andrew's Hall was rather reduced. The performance did not go well and on more than one occasion the choruses "degenerated into a noise".

Over the next few months further condemnation followed. Norwich Choral Society members were referred to as the "parasitic fungus" of the 1869 festival. The "incubus" by which the festival had been weighed down for many years, preventing it to prosper. They were accused of not being true amateurs, devoted to their art, because they accepted free tickets. This practice was regarded as "vampire like sucking the blood from the fountain from which it should have supplied".

By May 1870 James Frederick had resigned from his position as festival chorus master and on a Friday afternoon in May a meeting was held to select a new person for the post. Edward Bunnett*, Horace Hill and Henry Rudd put themselves forward for selection. Mr. Henry Rudd was unanimously elected to be the chorus master for the 1872 festival.

* Dr. Edward Bunnett at the time was assistant to Dr. Buck at Norwich Cathedral.

CHAPTER 22

Smallpox

As James Frederick and his chorus came to terms with their rebuff a tragedy befell the city. Sir Robert John Harvey Harvey, unbeknown to his partners at the Crown Bank had speculated unwisely and lost heavily. On 15th July 1870 in the grounds of his estate at Whitlingham, Sir Robert fired two pistol shots into his chest. One of the medics summoned was Dr. Copeman. For two days Sir Robert lingered before slipping into unconsciousness, dying on 19th July. On the morning of the 16th, customers of the bank had been greeted by locked doors bearing the following notice "Norwich Crown Bank. In consequence of the lamentable catastrophe which has happened to Sir Robert Harvey, it has been determined by the other partners to suspend the business of the bank at present". The same day a declaration of insolvency was signed by the other partners and the business transferred to Gurney's Bank. During the ensuing months the stock, contents and property of the Crown Point estate at Whitlingham were sold.

On 22nd November 1870 in St. Andrew's Hall another tragic event was highlighted. A Grand Monster Military concert by the bands of Carrow Works, the West Norfolk Militia, the 2nd Volunteer Artillery and the 1st Norfolk Volunteers with a choir of 60 singers was given in aid of funds for the widows and orphans of the officers and crew of H.M.S. "Captain". Although a modern ship it had capsized off Finisterre in September with the loss of many lives. The concert featured pieces with a nautical theme and included "The Sailor's Dream" sung by Mr. Minns. This disastrous year concluded with heavy snow fall with thick cloud cover which prevented the watching of the solar eclipse. Few would have noticed that for 3 minutes the sun was just visible as a brilliant crescent with its horns pointing down to Earth.

By the new year Henry Rudd had formed a chorus of 200 fresh voices, to whom he offered free singing tuition. This festival chorus proceeded to give 3 concerts during 1871. The first, in March, did not go well. The choruses on occasions were "all at sea"; Mr. Rudd "scarcely being master of the situation". The singers became confused as they could not hear the organ which warbled in its confined arch, acting as a "wet blanket". There was talk of returning the instrument to its original position for whilst it remained under the tower "no chorus in the world, however numerous or excellent" would do well in St. Andrew's Hall.

The principal singer in the October concert was Miss Marie Rosetti. This young blonde soprano with "lustrous" blue eyes, whose real name was Miss M. Brennan, was a native of Norwich. On the advice of Dr. Buck she had pursued her vocal studies in Italy. Although extremely nervous she showed capabilities. The performance of Mr. Lewis Thomas, the bass singer, however, was a disgrace. He "anticked" in a manner befitting a London music hall and was sharply reminded by the press that "vulgarity is not humour". Controversy still loomed over the amateur status of the festival chorus and band for each performer received 2 free tickets which were invariably sold. This was regarded as a form of payment. Of the 1500 people who attended the October concert 600 entered with gratis tickets. James Frederick's resignation had done little to settle the dispute.

Smallpox was in the city. People were becoming increasingly worried as the number of cases escalated. At the end of October the poor were furnished with free disinfectant. Householders had been instructed 8 weeks earlier to ensure all their servants had adequate vaccinations for it was unlawful to send infected servants home to their village. "Where the evil falls there it must be encountered". Parents were ordered not to transport the bodies of their dead children to the cemetery in cabs but to use the "proper vehicles". All burials took place within 48 hours of death. The disease continued to spread. All sorts of precautionary measures were taken. Carbolic acid was found to be useless and chlorine gas was recommended to disinfect and deodorise their homes. People were instructed to add vitriol to plates of common salt, then to hastily leave the room but before the cleansing could be done all gaps needed to be sealed and any bright irons or brasses securely wrapped in paper. Mr. Charles Cubitt, a chemist, (15) of 17 Market Place was so concerned that the disease was spread by the transfer of coinage, he insisted all his customers drop their money into a basin of disinfectant.

A special hospital for sufferers was erected on the outskirts of the city. The structure, brought from London, was lined with pitch pine, well ventilated and had many baths and nursing rooms. The hospital was run by Mr. and Mrs. Marjoram of London and Dr. Guy was appointed medical officer. It could cater for a maximum of 30 patients who could afford to pay the fee of 6/- per week. Deaths by smallpox continued to occur until July 1872.

The presence of the disease did not deter the Norwich Choral Society from holding their annual meeting on the first Monday in January 1872. Mr. Eaton had died on March 31st 1871 aged 71 years. The following tribute was recorded in the society's minutes "that this Society begs to record their testimony to the great loss sustained by them in the decease of the late President (T. D. Eaton) who had for many years most faithfully helped them through many difficulties by his great energy and musical talent and will long be remembered among them for his kindness of disposition, his cheerful and happy conversation and good fellowship". Mr. George Elward Simpson was elected as the new president. Conductor James Frederick offered his resignation to the society. He had wanted to step down at the 1871 annual meeting but was persuaded to continue for a further year. This time his resignation was accepted. For his "long and faithful service" he was made an honorary member of the society and an ex officio member of the committee. It was also unanimously agreed that he should be granted a gratuity of £20 per year in his retirement.

As a gesture of reconciliation with the festival committee, Mr. Henry Rudd was appointed conductor of the Norwich Choral Society. His tenure was short for he died suddenly at his Duke Street home on 14th March 1872 aged 51 years.

CHAPTER 23

Fire!

The festival committee allowed James Harcourt and his close friend Edward Bunnett to decide which of them would succeed Henry Rudd as Festival Chorus Master. The position was chosen by Harcourt with Bunnett taking over from Harcourt as festival organist. Much new music was planned for the 1872 festival. Macfarren composed a cantata "Outward Bound" the work portraying a ship on her farewell voyage. F. H. Cowen composed a "Festival Overture" and Benedict started to write a symphony in G minor but only two movements were completed in time. Edward Bunnett, at Benedict's suggestion composed "Rhineland", a cantata for solo, chorus and orchestra. A Duettino "Dunque mio bene" by J. Arthur Harcourt and an overture "Endymion" by King Hall were also to be performed for the first time. Hall was a pupil of the R. A. M. and had connections with Norwich by birth. Sullivan's "Te Deum", written to celebrate the recovery of the Prince of Wales from typhoid, and Benedict's oratorio "St. Peter", commissioned for the Birmingham festival the previous year were to be heard for the first time in Norwich.

The interior of St. Andrew's Hall took on a new appearance. The galleries no longer rose from the centre with equal gradation. Gone was the visual aspect of one mass of spectators. Instead the galleries elevated some distance above the ground, allowing the space beneath to provide seating for an extra 200 people. Under the west gallery Mr. Snelling provided a commodious refreshment saloon.

The usual soloists had been engaged with the addition of Mlle. Emma Albani. A week before the festival commenced a note arrived from Thomas Cutler M. D., physician to Mr. Sims Reeves. It read:- "I certify that Mr. Sims Reeves is quite unfit to fulfil his engagement at the Norwich Festival in consequence of catarrh and arthritic rheumatism". The singer had got thoroughly soaked whilst riding in an open carriage and caught a chill. Immediately the news was received Dr. Copeman travelled to Worcester to secure the services of Mr. Edward Lloyd. Lloyd commenced his journey to Norwich with fellow musicians from the west of England but their train was involved in an accident. Many instruments were destroyed. Luckily the artists were unscathed and continued their journey.

Edward Lloyd

Madame Albani

By the Tuesday evening of the festival Mde. Tietjens had developed a cold and after her poor performance retired to her sick bed. She reappeared on Thursday morning to sing in "St. Peter" but was clearly unwell however Mlle. Albani made up for everyone's disappointment for throughout the festival she sang with a voice of "delicious" quality, perfect in articulation and refinement of style.

The festival was well supported. The profit made allowed £500 to be given to charity.

On January 28th 1873 James Frederick's great friend Henry Hugo Pierson died in Leipzig. James Frederick had done much to promote his music. The original full score of his oratorio "Jerusalem" was thought to have been in James Frederick's handwriting.

His own health was deteriorating and he no longer appeared as an active member of Norwich's musical life.

Mr. Howlett's music business was thriving for he moved into new premises at the corner of London St. and the Walk. On Friday March 14th 1873, in a back room of the new shop, a dinner was laid on for all those involved in its erection. 80 guests enjoyed a meal provided by Mrs. Fountain of London St., afterwards songs and toasts enlivened the evening.

Two weeks later the shop of music dealer James Darken situated in London St., between Miller the tobacconist and Ralfe the silversmith, attracted a crowd of thousands as fire engulfed the property. At about 8 o'clock on a Saturday evening, shortly after the premises had been locked, smoke was observed coming from an upper window. It was immediately reported to the police station. The chief constable and Superintendent Barnard were soon at the scene accompanied by the fire brigade with the necessary equipment. The fire had taken hold in a second floor closet containing instruments and books. Access was difficult. Neighbouring properties were in danger but within 45 minutes the fire was under control. The sides and floor of the closet had burnt through. The rafters beneath, severely damaged allowing the contents of the closet to drop to the floor below. Several pianos fell into pieces, the heat causing the glue to melt. Smoke begrimed the walls and water damaged the contents of the lower floors. Staff had bravely removed the most valuable items to safety. The contents were insured by Norwich Union who paid the claim the following Monday. The building was owned by Mr. J. G. Johnson and whilst repairs were carried out Darken sold off his savaged stock at the former Crown Bank by kind permission of Messrs. Gurney & Co. Harmoniums, grand, bichord, and cottage pianos, manufactured by Broadwood, Collard, Hodgson & Ward, Alexandre, Caesarini and others could be bought at reduced prices. Sheet music continued to be sold from the London St. premises.

After Darken's sale rumours began to circulate that the Crown Bank building was to become the city's post office. The site was thought most unfavourable by some 30 tradesmen who, in October 1873, hastily signed a memorial to the Post Master General, voicing their concerns.

A week later a further letter was dispatched stating how the previous communicants were ignorant of the fact that a branch post office would remain in the city centre and in view of this they now supported the scheme. The second communication bore the names of about 100 tradesmen and respected city gentlemen including Zechariah Buck and Edward Bunnett.

In October 1873 London Street was again the focus of attention when Mr. Dixon displayed his "Norwich Time Ball" in the window of his shop. This electricial and mechanical devise received a signal each day at 1 o'clock direct from the Royal Observatory at Greenwich. It daily attracted a number of spectators some through curiosity and others eager to adjust their time pieces.

On Monday 15th June 1874 Dixon's shop was ravaged by fire. At 8 o'clock in the morning Mr. Dixon went to a little store room at the back of his home to get some oil to use about the works of the cathedral clock. He carried with him a lighted taper. Half an hour later smoke billowed from the upper windows of the property situated between Little London Street and Swan Lane (16). Dixon's wife, 2 children and servants were taken into the home of Mr. Fiske. Neighbour Mr. Caley, who owned the property, tackled the flames with small hoses kept on each floor of his house. By the time Superintendent Barnard, Inspector Curtis and the fire apparatus arrived, 3 streams of water already poured upon the flames but the fire still spread into the shop. Valuable clocks, watches, barometers and jewellery suffered severe damage. In consequence the items were sold off at much reduced prices and the Time Ball relocated in a temporary shop opposite Mr. Caley's premises.

Dixon resumed trading in his restored shop in January 1875. Above the window, was a new, large, red and gold Time Ball.

By 1875 James Frederick had moved from his St. Giles' Terrace home and was living at Point Cottage, Ipswich Rd, Norwich (17). On January 4th that year the Norwich Choral Society held their Annual General Meeting in St. Andrew's Hall. James Mottram was in the chair. He informed the meeting that something needed to be done to rectify the anomalous state of the society which for many years had only barely been alive. The committee were of the opinion that the wisest course of action was to wind up the society, leaving the meeting to decide how the funds should be distributed. The society had been in existence for 50 years and of late met just once a year to collect the 1/- subscription. The festival no longer engaged the choral society as one body; instead members were engaged as individuals, all but 5 of the society's 87 members being enrolled in the festival chorus.

Francis Sutton moved that the society should be wound up and the assets shared between its members. He felt the struggle to keep it afloat was not worth the effort. His motion was seconded by William Howlett. Not everyone was in agreement. Mr. Gostling thought the society should remain in a passive state. Its assets of £165-13s-6d plus any dividends from Harvey and Hudson's bankruptcy, being retained. If an emergency arose, the society could quickly be re-formed. Henry Thouless emphatically supported Gostling's view. He could see no reason why the society had to succumb to the forces of the festival. If at any time it was abandoned, with funds at hand, the society would be in a position to resuscitate itself and perhaps regain its former glory.

The motion to wind up the society was put to the vote. 50 were in favour, 14 against.

Mr. Gostling then proposed that £10 from the society's funds be donated to the Norwich Philharmonic Society in recognition of their valuable assistance over the past years. The motion, seconded by William Todd was put to the meeting. It lost by a large majority.

A proposal by R. Simpson that all the society's property, comprising of desks, forms, a harmonium and 2 complete oratorios should be realised and added to the funds for distribution, was seconded by Charles Noverre and put to the meeting. The members present voted on the dissolution of the Norwich Choral Society by 59 in favour, 4 against with 1 abstention.

A committee consisting of James Mottram, Mr. R. W. Ladell, George Brittain, Mr. A. J. Codling, and Mr. R. Simpson was formed to carry out the finalities.

The organisation to which James Frederick and his father had devoted much of their time and which had given so many memorable occasions was no more.

CHAPTER 24

Boom went the church of St. John.

The city was rather busy at the time of the 1875 festival. A horticultural meeting was taking place and another Royal Commission inquiry was in progress. The festival's programme did little to attract attention. The only unknown work was Sterndale Bennett's "Woman of Samaria". Bennett had died on 1st February 1875 and the work had been included as a tribute to his memory. It was felt by those present to be one of the heaviest dullest scores ever written. A selection from "Jerusalem" was also performed, in memory of Pierson.

Arthur Sullivan had been approached the previous February to compose a new work expressly for the festival. Payment was negotiated, a sum agreed and the cantata, "David and Jonathan" commenced. The first performance of the work was scheduled for the Thursday morning concert with the composer conducting. In July the committee received a letter from Sullivan explaining that due to overwork, he was unable to fulfil his promise. Rossini's "Stabat Mater" was therefore substituted in the programme. As usual the "Messiah" was performed on the Friday morning. After the completion of the first part, Benedict assembled the chorus in the Dutch Church. He was now aged 70 and had been festival conductor for 30 years. Although he could not anticipate events, he was of the mind that this would be his last opportunity to thank the singers and to say his farewells. He begged them to remember him as a true and faithful friend.

Attendance throughout the festival was low. Friday evening's ball attracted only 150 people and was subsequently discontinued.

The festival committee of late had been experiencing difficult times. Mr. F. J. Blake, the festival treasurer was seriously ill. His afflictions preventing him from attending the festival. Mlle. Albani kindly visited him at his King Street home where she partook of luncheon and favoured him by singing "The Last Rose of Summer". Blake died 2 months later, aged 75 years.

Not only had the committee to function without the services of their treasurer, but their secretary R. C. Gilman was still recovering from serious injuries sustained in the Thorpe rail crash on 10th September 1874 when 18 passengers and the crew of both locomotives had died in an horrific accident.

However the festival managed to make a small profit, all of

which was held in reserve. No money was given to the charities but Mlle. Albani generously donated 20 guineas to the Norfolk and Norwich and Jenny Lind hospitals.

In the week following the festival St. Andrew's Hall rang with the sound of young voices. A chorus of 600 pupils from various day schools performed in 2 concerts arranged by Mr. W. Howlett, who was then 73 years of age. Several Sankey and Moody hymns were sung to audiences of 1500 and 1350. A further treat was in store for the chorus on the Friday evening when Howlett gave a juvenile tea party in the hall. Having enthusiastically consumed a quantity of food the youngsters retired to the Dutch Church to enable the tables to be cleared. On return they found to their delight the tables had been relaid with all manner of desserts. At intervals throughout the party they raised their voices in song.

In February 1876 Joseph Joachim revisited the city. This time to appear in a concert arranged by Mr. Darken. The eminent violinist had been hurriedly engaged at considerable expense after Mde. Norman Neruda was compelled to withdraw through illness two weeks prior to the concert. Darken was congratulated on his most successful attempt to bring top quality music to Norwich.

On the evening of 13th September 1876 a terrifying boom echoed across the city. The sound, resembling cannon fire came from the church of St. John Maddermarket. Neighbouring houses shook from the blast. The church had recently been restored and was now lighted by gas standards. On this Wednesday evening the congregation departed after the evening service, leaving the Rev. H. L. Rumsey and members of the choir in the church for music practice. A smell of gas had been evident in the church for some little while but had been dismissed as not dangerous. The choir assembled on benches at the upper end of the north aisle by the vestry near to the organ. Additional light was required and Rev. Rumsey with lighted taper in hand proceeded to ignite the standard nearest to the pulpit. As he bent down to turn on the gas supply a brilliant streak of flame shot along the north side of the nave, instantly followed by the loud boom. Plunged into darkness the choir feared for their lives, but luckily escaped with only singed hair. The Rev. Rumsey was not so fortunate. He was hurled several yards across the church; his face cut and burnt; his arm broken and his beard and hair, singed. The gas standards had been wrenched and twisted. Benches turned into matchwood, their iron framework being flung with such force into the roof that pieces pierced the structure and dangled dangerously from above. The only glass which escaped the blast was that of the clock on the west wall.

James Frederick was now in extreme poor health. Throughout his long affliction he had never complained and still retained a genial disposition. All this time he had been faithfully attended to by his friend Alfred Master* On 9th February 1877 at his Point Cottage home, James Frederick died.

Although he had composed little during his life, his works were models of musical correctness. He had carried out the choral arrangements for 9 triennial festivals and despite being severely strict at rehearsals, was loved by all. The principles from London often remarked how they "felt safe with him". With a few picked voices he had regularly attended the festivals at Birmingham, Worcester, Gloucester and Hereford. On 2 occasions he had been summoned to Windsor Castle by Her Majesty Queen Victoria to entertain the Royal party after supper.

The body of James Frederick was committed to the family plot on the Rosary on 11th February 1877. It was a very quiet affair according to his wishes.

Alfred Master FRCS was surgeon to the County gaol and a prominent member of the Norfolk and Norwich Festival committee. (2)

1=Blyth Borwich directory 1842
2= Norfolk Annals
3= NRO SO33/5
4= NRO SO33/6
5= 1858 Postal Directory of Cambridge/Norfolk/Suffolk
6= PRO 1851 census index, document 1815/412
7= NRO MS21197
8= NRO SO33/7
9= White's directory of Norfolk1854
10= NRO N/TC6/3
11= White's directory of Norfolk 1864
12= White's directory of Norfolk 1845
13= NRO SO33/8
14= NRO SO 33/9
15= Harrod's directory of Norwich 1868
16= Hamilton's directory of Norwich 1879
17= Postal directory of Norfolk 1875
All other information from the "Norwich Mercury", the "Norfolk Chronicle" and the "Annals of the Norfolk and Norwich Triennial Musical Festivals" by R. H. Legge and W. E. Hansell published by Jarrold in 1896.

PART III

HORACE HILL

CHAPTER 25

Horace at Wymondham.

Horace was born on the 23rd August 1832. In 1841 he lived in Cow Hill with his father John, aged 40; mother Sarah aged 40; elder sister Elizabeth, elder brothers Emanual and Henry, and baby brother Alfred. (1). His 24 year old brother James Frederick, had begun his musical career.

The festival of 1845 had the services of two H. Hills in the chorus; one singing alto the other second treble each receiving the sum of £1-0s-0d, (2). Horace's mother had died just 3 months previous, on 15th June 1845. At the age of 13 Horace was orphaned, his father John dying on 28th July 1846.

During the next 2 years Horace fell in love with Pricilla Appleton Clark whose father taught music in Ten Bell Lane (3) and on 31st August 1848 they married in St. Gregory's church Norwich (4). She was several years his elder. At the time of their marriage Horace was residing in the parish of St Swithin's and was himself a teacher of music. (4). The musical festival was only 2 weeks away and rehearsals were long and frequent. Horace was playing "oboes" in the festival band for which he received the sum of £3-3s-0d. (2).

By 1850 Pricilla's father had moved to 98 Pottergate (5) but it is unknown where Horace and Pricilla spent their first 2 years of married life. However, by 1851 Horace had become a professor of music and was living in accommodation in the vicinity of the "Dukes Palace" with his wife and 2 young daughters Emeline Jane and Harriet Elizabeth. (6).

The festival of 1852 found Horace again playing oboes, receiving this time only £3-0s-0d (7). His ability to teach was soon recognised and by 1858 he had moved to 53 Pottergate St and built up a teaching schedule around the county. On Tuesdays he visited North Walsham and Knapton; the villages of Little Melton, Carlton, Barford and Crownthorpe on Wednesdays, Wymondham on Thursdays and Bixley on Saturdays.

Six months later his weekly teaching rota had changed and his place of residence had become 45 Pottergate St. He continued to teach at North Walsham and Knapton on Tuesdays but on

Wednesdays he taught at Shropham and Wymondham; Thursdays, Hingham, Kimberley and Barford and on Mondays, Fridays and Saturdays he taught in Norwich.

Through his travelling Horace became involved with various musical concerts within the county. On 18th February 1859 he conducted a concert in North Walsham Town Hall directed by the principal and masters of the Collegiate School. The 14 performers included Mr. Proops and Mr. F. Hill. Featured in the programme was an overture composed by Horace which received loud applause.

During 1859 Horace became the Bandmaster to the Volunteer Rifle Corps Band. Norwich being one of the first places to form such a band. In January 1860 the Norwich Choral Society entrusted the bandmaster with the trumpet obligato part to "The Trumpet Shall Sound" in their performance of the "Messiah". A thousand people filled St. Andrew's Hall expecting this part of the performance to be a disappointment. Mr. Harper usually took this part but his demand of a 7 guineas fee proved too expensive for a 1/- concert. The audience was however pleasantly surprised for Horace's splendid interpretation on the brass clarionet was far superior to the alternatives available of either the organ stop or a valve trumpet.

Horace's volunteer band rehearsed frequently. Their talent was shown to the public on 21st February 1860, when 50 performers gave a concert in St. Andrew's Hall. The coaching and unretiring efforts of their bandmaster being recognised by the 1200 people who braved the cold and miserable weather to attend. The men, dressed in uniform, presented an unusual exciting appearance in the hall and the selection of music was of admirable good taste. The stirring martial spirit of the "Evening Drum" accompanied by a "Lilliputian" drummer caused such a sensation that an encore was demanded.

The Rifle Corps dinner was held in St. Andrew's Hall in May. Thick evergreens embraced the front porch. Inside the scent of flowers filled the hall, whilst banners, crimson drapery and pieces of armour decorated the pillars. 510 people sat down to a meal with excellent wines, provided by Mr. Heseltine of the Royal Hotel. The band, conducted by Horace, entertained with the playing of spirited tunes in a very creditable manner. Horace was praised for creating a band worthy of the corps and the city.

In July the band lost its first member: Volunteer George T.

Hewitt aged 20 years. At 8.30 on the morning of Sunday 15th July 1860, 300 uniformed men assembled at St. Giles' Gate under the command of Captain Hay Gurney. 12 volunteers carrying their arms in reverse, led the funeral procession, followed by the band playing the "Dead March" from "Saul". As the hearse and mourning coach proceeded to the Rosary cemetery, the lines of uniformed men on each side of the street fell in behind, four abreast. A large group of spectators gathered at the graveside*. 3 volleys were fired each preceded by a drum roll, as the body of Volunteer George T. Hewitt was laid to rest. The men then marched back to Foundry Bridge where they were dismissed.

At this time Horace also held the position of music teacher at Wymondham Grammar School, in Middleton Street, under the headmastership of the Rev. Joseph Grisdale. On a Wednesday evening in December 1860 the school gave their 3rd annual concert in the schoolroom. The room had been festively decorated with flags and festoons of ivy, holly and mistletoe. An excellent programme of music was given under the direction of Horace which reflected great credit on his ability. 3 deafening cheers were given to the Rev. and Mrs. Grisdale and after supper the evening concluded with dancing.

The December weather of 1860 was bitter but this did not deter Horace and the Norwich Rifle Band travelling to Wymondham for the town's Rifle Corps inspection. Lord Wodehouse had been invited to perform the task. Snow fell heavily as the company assembled at the drill ground and as they marched to the Market Place became quite deep under foot. At 1 o'clock several people gathered to watch the men line up in front of the King's Head Hotel for inspection. Despite the atrocious conditions, it was evident great progress had been made in their training. The Norwich Rifle Corps band, led by Horace then played "God Save the Queen". In the evening Horace's band gave a concert in the Drill Room.

Further band concerts were held in Norwich at the beginning of the new year under the baton of Horace. An admission charge of 3d was made to the general public whilst men in uniform were allowed free entry.

In March the band, assisted by the band of the 10th Hussars, performed a lively selection of music in St. Andrew's Hall opening with Mendelssohn's "Wedding March" The second part of the programme included the "Norwich Volunteers Galop" composed by their talented bandmaster, Horace Hill who in a short space of time had brought them to a point of excellence.

The year concluded with another Christmas concert at Wymondham Grammar School. This time the musical entertainment included "Dixie Polka" composed by Horace. In recognition of the school's respect for their music master, an elder pupil presented Horace with a superb gold Albert chain.

By 1862 Horace and his family had returned to Cow Hill for on 13th May 1862, at their home, his beloved wife, Pricilla, died aged 35 years. On the 16th she was buried on Earlham Cemetery.* in a common grave.

* George T. Hewitt's grave. Rosary Cemetery Plot G 4/1210
* Pricilla Hill's grave Earlham cemetery Section 8/670.

CHAPTER 26

Horace and Mary

Horace continued teaching piano and singing with the addition of concertina and harmonium tuition. In January 1863 his profession took him to Beeston Hall, Smallburgh, Knapton, North Walsham, Aylsham, Thorpe Market, Wymondham and Thetford.

He became attracted to Mary Grisdale, the daughter of the headmaster of Wymondham Grammar School; she was several years his junior. They married on 24th June 1863 at Wymondham Abbey. The Rev. Robert Eden officiated. (8)

Horace and Mary resided at St. Stephen's Gate, Norwich and by January 1864 Antingham Rectory, Cawston and Reepham, Knapton House, North Walsham, and Ketteringham were included in his teaching itinerary.

On Tuesday 28th April 1864 the Norwich Harmonic Society gave their 6th concert in the Lecture Room in St. Andrew's. Mr. Wurr, the founder of the society, conducted a programme of vocal and instrumental music. A song composed by Horace, "Sweet Summer Time" was sung most successfully by Miss Cunningham.

The following evening Horace took part in the 47th Norwich Philharmonic Society concert in the Noverre Room. This evening of vocal and instrumental music featured works by Haydn, Handel, Beethoven and an aria from Pierson's "Faust". A comic song "The Accomplished Young Lady" was sung by Horace but his voice lacked the power to be heard at the back of the room. The concert was considerably lengthened by numerous encores.

One of Horace's duties at this time was Professor of Music at Miss C. Boyden's Establishment for Young Ladies at 58 Pottergate St. As well as music, the young ladies were instructed in dancing by Mr. Noverre and French by Mons. Reily. The Establishment moved to the more commodious premises of 66 Pottergate St. in October 1864.

In 1865 Horace took over from Mr. John T. Mower as organist at North Walsham parish church. Mr. Mower resigned after a disagreement, having held the post for 44 years. Horace's connections with the locality resulted in him forming a Musical Society in the town in 1868 (9). He was rapidly gaining recognition as an arranger/composer. At the 54th Norwich Philharmonic concert on 15th April 1868 ample justice was done by the band to his well arranged "Pot Pourri for orchestra".

H. Hill junior and C. Noverre assisted with the vocal items. A few weeks later Horace's quartet "Morning Song" was performed in the 14th Norwich Vocal Society concert conducted by his brother James Frederick.

The Church of England Young Men's Society acquired an excellent new harmonium for their St. Peter's St. rooms and on 30th April 1868 Horace played the instrument to entertain the 50 members who had gathered for their half yearly tea. On 2nd December his talents as a composer were brought to the fore when on this Wednesday evening a concert compiled nearly entirely of his own music, was given in the Noverre Room. Mayor Harvey was amongst the relatively large audience. Part 1 commenced with a sacred cantata and service in F, both of his own pen. The cantata opened with a spirited introduction and fugue in G minor. The fine choruses "Gracious is the Lord" and "O Praise Our God" were followed by a beautifully melodious quartet "He is Blessed". Mr. Smith sang the spirited air for bass "While I Live I Will Praise Thee Lord" which was in a minor mode and a lovely duet for soprano and tenor "Cause Me To Hear Thy Loving Kindness In The Morning" was sung by Miss Spiller and Mr. Metcalf. The work concluded with an unaccompanied quartet "Sing Unto God" which was afterwards taken up by the chorus ending in a florid fugue on the words "So I Will Always Sing Praise Unto Thy Name. Amen". The audience was delightfully astonished with the beauty and effectiveness of the composition. Although at times it showed signs of being influenced by various great composers it also proved Horace to be a vigorous musical thinker. The work was deemed worthy of a place in the festival.

His service in F, a composition of "unusual merit", had previously been performed in the Catholic Chapel.

Horace conducted both works admirably and on their completion had to return several times to the platform to acknowledge the loud and prolonged applause. The second part of the concert opened with a wedding march by Horace which was excellently played and encored. "The Calm" met with a similar success as did his song "I Love the Bright Sunny light" sung by Miss Spiller, who also conceded to an encore. Pierson's "Ye Mariners of England" brought the entertainment to a close.

In the large room of the Free Library on the evening of Friday 26th February 1869, Horace conducted the St Simon's church choir. The concert was under the management of Miss A. E.

Warnes, who earlier in the evening had supplied the members of the choir with a sumptuous tea. For the greater part of this concert of sacred music Horace presided at the harmonium. A harmonium and piano duet with Miss E. A. Wright was well received as was his own anthem "How Great is the Lord". During the interval plentiful refreshments were available and Miss Warnes, on behalf of the choir, Miss Wright and herself, presented Horace with a gold telescopic pencil case in recognition of his gratuitous service in training the choir. This handsome gift bore the inscription "Horace Hill February 26th 1869" with the monogram H. H. on a stone.

On 31st March Horace was back in the large room of the Free Library. This time Shakespeare's play "The Tempest" was being read, interspersed with musical interludes by the band and chorus of the Free Christian Church conducted by Horace Hill Mus. Bac. He had only recently gained his degree from St. John's College, Cambridge (10). The play was read by the Rev. J. Crompton, Messrs. J. R. Sawyer, J. S. Bird, H. J. Booty, R. W. Ladell, T. Andrews, W. N. Cooper, F. Ellingham and W. Stevens.

On the morning of Thursday 2nd September 1869 Horace's cantata was granted the honourable position of being performed before Rossini's "Messe Solennelle" in the festival concert. Horace took up the baton in front of a fairly filled hall. The patrons stalls were crowded with a fashionable assembly of county families including Lord Stafford and Lord Suffield. Since its first performance the work had been "added to and improved". The beautiful quartet "He is Blessed" was admirably sung by Mlle. Tietjens, Mde. Patey, Mr. Cummings and Mr. Santley. At its conclusion rapturous applause from both the audience and the orchestra resounded through the hall. Horace had composed a work which had given immense pleasure and was believed to be a valuable addition to the sacred cantata repertoire.

CHAPTER 27

St. Giles' Church

In 1870 Horace failed to secure the position of festival chorus master left vacant by the resignation of his elder brother, James Frederick.

His routine carried on as before until 7th January 1871 when he conducted a Grand Concert in St. Andrew's Hall in aid of St. Paul's church organ fund. Miss Cunningham, Mr. Smith and Mr. Minns were the soloists in this concert of sacred and secular music. The weather was poor; the attendance, fair. Horace's home in St. Stephen's Gate now rang with the sound of children's voices for Mary had produced sons Horace, Alfred and Claud and daughter Edith. They employed 19 year old Elizabeth Holmes as a servant (11).

In June 1871 Horace was appointed organist of St. Giles' church, Norwich, following the resignation of Mr. John Fox (12). He received a salary of £25 per year which had to be raised by voluntary subscription. The amounts collected varied between 10/6d and 1 guinea with the rector, the Rev. W. N. Ripley giving a generous £5.

The church had been extensively restored in 1866 at a cost of £4000, £1000 of which came from the Rev. W. N. Ripley (13). A chancel was added and a new organ costing £350, by Hill of London, was erected on the north side (13). The graves in the churchyard had been levelled in 1868; the headstones being placed on the surface. Trees and shrubs were planted and the walkways gravelled. The choir of St. Giles gave a concert in the school room in January 1872. It had only been formed 6 month but "too much praise can not be given to the organist Horace Hill for the skill and attention displayed in its training". Horace's anthems "O Sing unto the Lord" and "Great is the Lord" as well as a duet "The Wind", featured in the programme along with works by Pierson, Rossini, Benedict and Farmer. The playing of "God Save the Queen" brought the concert to a close.

Two new musical societies had been established in the city the previous November. The Gate House Choir, a part song and madrigal group of around 40 members was led by Henry Rudd and the Norwich Musical Union formed by Dr. Edward Bunnett, Mons. Oury and Horace Hill. Some felt this society was in direct opposition to that of Henry Rudd, although a leaflet advertising

St Giles Church before restoration

Reproduced by kind permission of the Norfolk Record Office

its formation stated quite clearly that it had no wish to clash with any existing societies.

The inauguration concert of the Norwich Musical Union took place on 18th April 1872. Its 150 performers delighting a crowded St Andrew's Hall with their performance of Barnett's cantata "The Ancient Mariner". Horace assisted Edward Bunnett with the conducting. One of the soloists was Miss Bessie Hill, Horace's daughter. She possessed a sweet toned but not powerful soprano voice and sang her part splendidly. The singers rehearsed in the Clerical Rooms in the Lower Close. Their second concert was given on 12th December. Horace presided at the organ and Edward Bunnett conducted Benedict's "St. Cecilia" which filled the first part of the programme. The miscellaneous second part featured Mendelssohn's cantata "To the Sons of Art" and a violin duet in C minor by Mayseder, played by Oury and his pupil Mr. H. Tuddenham. Both works had never been performed in Norwich. The proceeds from the concert were given to Oury who was in the process of establishing a music club called the "Corelli Club". They intented to meet in Mr Howlett's new music room which was being constructed on the corner of London St. and the Walk. The club would offer gentlemen the opportunity of weekly practice under Oury's personal direction.

The inaugural concert of the North Walsham Amateur Musical Society was given in January 1873. The society was under the patronage of Lord and Lady Suffield, Hon. and Mrs Harbord Harbord, Admiral the Hon. and Mrs. E. Thornton Wodehouse, Sir E. Lacon Bart. M. P., The Hon. F. Walpole M. P., Sir H. and Lady Robinson, J. Petre esq, and Col. and Mrs. Duff. This concert of sacred and secular music was conducted by Horace Hill. "Too much praise cannot be given to the conductor Horace Hill Mus. Bac. for the energy he has displayed in bringing the first concert of the North Walsham Music Society to such a brilliant success". The programme included a performance of the "William Tell Overture" effectively rendered by 4 ladies on 2 pianos. Pierson's "God Shall Wipe Away" and Blumenthal's song "A Day Dream" were sung most charmingly by Bessie Hill. The concert raised £30 towards the purchase of a new organ for the parish church.

Horace's skills were becoming increasingly in demand. In February 1873 he conducted a concert given by the Carrow Singing Class, in aid of funds for the orphans home. This vocal and instrumental concert took place in the Carrow School Room.

Sterndale Bennett's "The May Queen" occupied the first part. Their performance reflected great credit on Horace and showed the immense care and attention he had bestowed in preparing this work. Bessie sang the role of the May Queen and Mr. Minns, the Lover. In the miscellaneous second part Bessie and Mr. Minns sang a duet "When the Silver Snow is Falling" and Bessie's solo "A Day Dream" received considerable applause. Throughout the evening Mr. R. S. C. Keymer presided at the piano. His playing of a solo "La Rosée du Matin" composed by Horace delighted the well filled room to such an extent that an encore was given.

Bessie's talents were also being recognised. In April she sang in one of Mr Herbert Anderson's Wednesday evening concerts in the King's Head Hotel at Wymondham where she charmingly sang Macfarren's "My Sailor Lad". Two weeks later she was singing at Diss for the first time, in one of the choral society's concerts. She astonished her audience. "The lady's voice has an extraordinary compass which was brought out almost to perfection".

The following spring Bessie made a similar impression when she performed at North Walsham. The Amateur Musical Society concert in the National School Room was conducted by her father and again raised funds for a new church organ.

CHAPTER 28

Paston Grammar School

In the spring of 1874 Horace occupied the position of music teacher at Paston Grammar School receiving a fee for that term of £2-12s-6d. and £3-6s-8d for subsequent terms (14). The school had reopened in February 1874 after extensive modernisation costing £1200, under the headmastership of the Rev. F. Pentreath. It educated 31 boys who paid between £4 and £8 for tuition in a wide range of subjects in addition to boarding fees of £25 to £30 per year. (14) The school's water and drainage systems had been made as effective possible and each room had a gas supply.

In the December the boys gave a concert to raise funds for the school library, under the able direction of their "indefatigable instructor Horace Hill".

The North Walsham Amateur Musical Society gave another concert in January 1875. This time the society was raising funds for the parish church roof. Horace conducted and his friends from Norwich came to assist. James Harcourt played the harmonium and Oury led the band which was "almost entirely" compiled of Norwich musicians. The first half of the evening's programme was parts 1 and 2 of the "Creation", the singers reflecting great credit upon themselves and the excellent training of their instructor, Horace Hill.

Paston Grammar School

The 31st March 1875 was a great occasion in North Walsham. Their new church organ, erected by Messrs. Hill and Son of London at a cost of £487 was opened by James Turle, organist of Westminster Abbey. This 2 manual instrument, placed in the north aisle of the chancel had a case made of plain pine with an ornamented diapered front. The great manual consisted of an open diapason 8ft; dulciana 8ft; stopped diapason 8ft; principal 4ft; waldflöte 4ft; fifteenth; 3 rank mixture and trumpet 8ft. The swell had an open diapason 8ft; hohlflöte 8ft; principal 8ft; oboe 8ft; cornopean 8ft and piccolo 2ft. The pedal division had only an open diapason 16ft. There were 3 couplers and 3 composition pedals. Space had been left for a clarionet on the great; a dulciana, twelfth and fifteenth on the swell and a bourdon on the pedals, when funds permitted. The organ's inauguration took the form of 2 services. 1300 people flocked to the first of these in the afternoon. Several members of the Rev. J. S. Owen's former parish, St. Matthew's, Norwich, had made the journey by the new rail link which had opened the previous October.

For his opening voluntary Turle played "I Know My Redeemer Liveth". The sermon was preached by the Dean of Norwich. The hymn "Praise my Soul the King of Heaven" was sung to a special tune by John Goss and "Angel Voices" to a tune by A. S. Sullivan. The service concluded with Turle playing Handel's "Coronation Anthem". The collection amounted to £39-13s-5½d. The evening congregation was not so large and the collection amounted to just £9-11s-11¾d. With donations, a total of £60 was raised that day for the organ fund.

Walter Lain was appointed organist of the new instrument. The gentleman had recently become organist to the Norwich Musical Union. Horace continued his musical association with the town. In the Musical Society's April concert, Mr. Wilkins, Mr. Burton and Horace Hill played a trio by Reissiger.

June 17th 1875 was prize day at Paston Grammar. The school had been "prettily" decorated for the occasion. A large assemblage witnessed the awarding of prizes for Divinity, Greek, Latin, History, Geography, French, Mathematics etc. by the High Sheriff of Norfolk, Sir T. Fowell Buxton Bart. Horace had assisted with the arrangements for a concert of recitations and musical pieces to entertain the guests and accompanied the singing on the harmonium. The whole performance was "exceedingly well executed".

The headmaster, Mr. Pentreath, had been recovering from an accident. On a Wednesday afternoon in early May the gentleman, his wife and 2 children were driving out in a pony carriage when the animal took fright at the corner of the hill leading from the town near Messrs. Loads' shop. It slipped on a piece of harness; became unmanageable and rushed furiously towards the Angel Hotel, opposite to which the cart overturned, dashing its occupants to the ground. Although the children suffered only minor injuries, Mr. and Mrs. Pentreath were much bruised and shaken from their ordeal.

As the year progressed Edward Bunnett had a set of 3 piano pieces published by Novello and Co. Entitled "The Rose", "The Thistle" and "The Shamrock" he had dedicated them to the Duke of Connaught. The festival, under the chorus training of James Harcourt, came and went without any signs of Horace taking part and Prince's Street congregational church acquired a splendid new organ built by Willis.

A new form of entertainment was sweeping the city; the Spelling Bee quiz. One such quiz in January 1876 had musical interludes performed by Edward Bunnett, his son Arthur and Walter Lain. In May Mr. Dixon exhibited a novelty clock in his shop. At each hour folding doors beneath the dial revealed a flautist who played a short melody before retreating.

On a June Sunday evening people congregated outside St. Giles' church, it being so densely crowded within. The Rev. W. S. Rainford, curate of the church, was preaching his farewell sermon. He was leaving for America where he would assist the New York Episcopalian clergyman the Rev. Dr. Lyng. The previous Friday Rainford's friends had presented him with a gold watch as a parting gift.

Just prior to Christmas Horace concluded 1876 by conducting a concert in Diss Corn Hall. Bessie Hill and Miss Emily Harcourt had also made the journey to take part. Since its formation Diss Choral Society, under the baton of Horace, had performed Mozart's 12th Mass, Haydn's "Creation", Costa's "Eli" and a motett by Horace "Hear Us O King of Heaven". Michael Costa had written to the society, expressing how glad he was to learn that they had distinguished themselves in the performance of his work. "I congratulate them all and thank everybody for the interest they have taken in my work. I also congratulate your talented conductor, Mr. Hill for the well deserved success of his motett".

The Annual General Meeting of the Diss Choral Society was held in the Magistrate's Room at the 30th January 1877. Horace's brother James Frederick was only days away from death. At 6 o' clock on this Tuesday evening the society partook of a capital tea provided by Mr. E Weavers, after which they adjourned to the Corn Hall so the tables could be cleared. On return they found them laden with delicious desserts. Among the votes of thanks given during the evening, was one to their conductor Horace Hill.

It was the start of another successful year for the Diss and North Walsham musical societies under the excellent training of Horace; Bessie's beautiful voice being heard on several occasions.

The North Walsham Society concert in April was hampered by a severe thunderstorm which passed over the region at 7 o'clock and considerably reduced the attendance. In this same month Diss Choral Society performed part of Haydn's "Seasons" as well as a varied selection of other pieces before a large and appreciative audience. Included was a duet sung from manuscript by Miss Walker and Mr. Reeder of a cantata composed by Horace. Several musicians had travelled from Norwich to augment the band. Mr. Hemstock presided at the organ and also assisted with the conducting. Horace accompanied on the piano. The success of the concert caused the press to comment that "Horace Hill must feel highly gratified with the marked improvement manifest in the Society".

CHAPTER 29

The Rejection of Edward Bunnett

Zechariah Buck, tendered his resignation at the cathedral on 5th June 1877. His long service terminating in September when, in poor health, he left Norwich to spend the remaining months of his life with his son, Henry, in Newport, Essex.

Horace's friend and colleague Edward Bunnett, had been Buck's assistant for 28 years and it was widely assumed that he would accede to the position. Dean Goulburn however had other plans and appointed Mr. Thomas Craddock. Craddock was organist at Torquay and had formerly been organist at St. John Paddington where the Dean had been vicar.

Zechariah Buck

Edward Bunnett

The musical world of Norwich and beyond became incensed at the rejection of Dr. Bunnett. Craddock, aware of the discontent, wrote to the Dean asking to be liberated from his engagement owing to "The immense amount of hostility displayed by the inhabitants of Norwich and Norfolk". Craddock was also of the opinion "that Dr. Bunnett had been sorely used".

With the position again vacant, it was hoped the Dean would reconsider Dr. Bunnett, but on 9th November 1877 it was announced that Dr. F. E. Gladstone was to be the new organist choirmaster of Norwich Cathedral.

Bunnett was devastated. Many sympathised with his plight, so a Complimentary Concert was arranged by his friends and fellow musicians for 28th November 1877. It was hoped the concert would compensate in some way for his bitter disappointment. The mayor Mr. J. D. Smith, the sheriff Mr. H. Bullard, the deputy mayor R. Coller, the ex deputy mayor E. K. Harvey, the ex sheriff W. Cadge; J. J. Colman M.P.; C. S. Read M.P; Sir Henry Robinson; Lady Bayning; F. Hay Gurney, and J. B. Morgan, all became patrons. Horace Hill, Kingston Rudd, James Mottram and Alfred Master were among 60 people who pledged their support. Sir Julius Benedict offered his services to conduct free of charge. Messrs. Broadwood & Sons and Messrs. W. Howlett & Sons generously loaned grand pianos entirely without cost. The Norfolk and Norwich Musical Union, the Gate House Choir and leading operatic soloists kindly offered their assistance. The local press allowed free advertising in their column.

On the evening of 28th St. Andrew's Hall was full. Bunnett's cantata "Lora" and his part song "Beware" formed part of the programme. 1109 people paid admission to the hall and a profit was made of £130. Bunnett expressed how exceedingly touched he was by the great kindness shown towards him from all quarters of society.

In the week prior to Christmas, Horace attended Dr. Bunnett's formal presentation in the Guildhall. After an elegant luncheon the mayor handed over a purse of 130 sovereigns and an illuminated address. Julius Benedict sent his apologies, unable to be present owing to professional duties in Hull.

At that time Horace was preparing for his mus. doc. examination at Cambridge for on the 5th January 1878, it was announced that he had successfully gained his degree. To obtain this title he had composed "Supplication and Praise", an 8 part work comprising of an overture written in the form of a symphonic first movement, a terzetto in open canon form, a quintett in strict canon form, a recit and air for tenor voice, an arioso for contralto voice, a duet for soprano and tenor on a ground bass, a quartett and a double fugue in 8 parts. The candidate also had to write an analysis of Mozart's Requiem and attend an examination at Cambridge.

Before the 1878 music festival the roof of St. Andrew's Hall had been extensively restored. The gaudy stucco substituted for stained timbers. A new orchestra was constructed for £300, the cost being shared between the council and the festival committee.

Mr. Hay Gurney had succeeded Dr. Copeman as chairman of the committee, following his retirement in 1876 and a new chorus of volunteers formed. Initially the rules stated that there would be no payment whatsoever to the chorus members, but before a sufficient number of voices came forward, this rule had to be modified. The chorus master was Harcourt with Bunnett as festival organist. Benedict was again the festival conductor, but some felt he was really too old for the position.

There was no concert on Monday evening so the "cheap" price admission charges were transferred to the Tuesday evening. The only unknown work in the whole festival was Macfarren's "Joseph" which had been written for the Leeds Festival the previous year.

"Joseph" was performed on the Wednesday morning. The work was 2¾ hours long and was followed by Mozart's 1st Mass. The audience grew tired; the chorus exhausted and everyone was relieved when the final chord sounded.

The Friday evening ball was replaced with another reduced price concert. This sudden addition to the programme caused a rush for tickets and the hall was crammed full. At the conclusion of the concert, Benedict was showered with flowers by the ladies of the chorus. During the afternoon he had again assembled the performers in the Dutch church. This time for a presentation to James Harcourt of a marble clock and to Edward Bunnett, an epergne, in recognition to their services to music.

About 2 weeks later the city experienced a heavy snow fall. Its rapid thaw followed by continuous rain coincided with a high tide. The height of the river Wensum rose dramatically causing many low lying city streets to be flooded. Hundreds of people were forced to leave their homes and a temporary refuge was set up in the disused governor's house at the old city gaol. (13)

Every Friday afternoon during the winter months Horace gave free elementary tuition to pupils attending the parochial schools of St. Stephen's, Norwich. These lectures were held in Crook's Place and on the evening of 19th December 1878, the students set an examination which Horace had devised. The results were disclosed at a meeting held in the Girls' School Room, Crooks Place on a Friday afternoon in March 1879. The Rev. James Wilson M.A. chaired the meeting. He praised Horace for the great attention and care he had taken in his instruction and then called upon him to give his report which read "My examination paper given on Friday evening 19th December contained 12 questions some of which were difficult to solve. It is therefore gratifying to find that H. Grix, to whom I have awarded the first prize, satisfactorily answered 10 of those questions. The answers given by the other candidates were not quite so satisfactory but I am pleased to award 3 other prizes. The second to R. Grix. The third to E. S. Grix and the forth to Albert W. Bartram.....". Horace then went on to thank the clergy for their attendance during the examination. Mrs Wilson distributed the prizes of "nicely bound" editions of Banister's excellent work on "Music" and a copy of Handel's "Messiah" to the successful candidates. Each prize contained a certificate of efficiency on the fly leaf signed by the Examiner, Dr. Horace Hill.

The first performance of a new oratorio entitled "Nehemiah" was given by Diss Choral Society in April 1879. The Corn Hall was full with leading families of the district who had come to hear this 1½ hour work composed by "our clever fellow citizen" Horace Hill. Horace had based his libretto on the book of the Bible bearing the same name and clothed it with appropriate music. Despite only one full rehearsal the 70 strong band and chorus performed the oratorio most competently; a testimony to their excellent training. Bessie Hill, Miss A. L. Moore, Mr. Minns, Mr. Shelford Cole, Mr. W. J. Foxell and Mr. F. Aldrich took the solo parts. An unaccompanied quartett "Wherefore is Thy Soul Cast Down?", a cleverly written canon "Commit Thy Way Unto the Lord" and a tenor air "O Lord Thou Hast Searched Me" were thought to be the most charming features of the work and deserved popularity in their own right. The whole work was so well written, it was considered worthy of a place in the next festival. This evening of delightful music concluded with the "Hallelujah" from "Engedi", an English version of the "Mount of Olives".

CHAPTER 30

A new organ for St. Andrew's Hall

The organ in St. Andrew's Hall had been allowed to deteriorate into a deplorable state. The noises it now produced embarrassed both player and listener to such an extent the instrument was declared a disgrace to the city. On Friday 7th November 1879 a meeting was held at the home of Charles Noverre to discuss the way forward. Dr. Horace Hill, Dr. Bunnett, Dr. Gladstone, Dr. Copeman, H. G. Barwell, J. Harcourt, W. Howlett, J. Mottram, H. K. Rudd, F. Sutton, and F. O.Taylor were among those present. Here they agreed to approach the organ builders Bryceson Bros. and Ellis, of Charlton Works, Islington who would inspect the space available, draw up a specification and propose a cost for a new instrument.

A deputation met Mayor Bullard in the New Year. A committee was set up and the mayor started a subscription fund for the organ by donating £100. Large sums were also received from J. J. Colman, J. H. Tillett, the Duke of Norfolk, Lord Stafford, Lord Suffield, Sir R. J. Buxton, Edward Birkbeck, and the Bishop of Norwich. Over the next few months the list of subscribers steadily grew showing the Rev. W. N. Ripley adding £20; James Mottram, 10 guineas; J. Darken, 10 guineas; Messrs. Howlett, 5 guineas; Dr. Bunnett, 3 guineas; Dr. Gladstone, 2 guineas; Julius Benedict, 2 guineas; Dr. Horace Hill, 2 guineas; Walter Lain, 1 guinea and J. Harcourt, 1 guinea.

In April 1880 the mayor staged a "novelty" entertainment entitled "National Scenes and National Melodies", in St. Andrew's Hall for 3000 children from elementary schools. Views of Scotland, Wales, Ireland and England supplied by Mr. E.G. Wood of Cheapside, London; were exhibited on a 20 foot wide screen by the best lanterns obtainable. The young audience sat through 12 slides of Wales, 15 of Ireland, 13 of Scotland and 16 of England interspersed with characteristic melodies from each country. These popular songs were performed by a choir of 500 juvenile and adult voices, under the direction of Alfred Gaul, accompanied by a military band. Gaul had assisted with 6 similar events in Birmingham but it was the first of its kind in Norwich. The juvenile section of the chorus had been instructed by Mr. Leader of the Boys Model School and Mr. Wilson of Surrey Rd. Boarding School. All wore cardinal red rosettes and had red covers to their

135

song books. They were supported by 60 adults from the festival chorus who took up a central position on the orchestra. Their rosettes of Cambridge blue also matched their book covers. The "Men of Harlech", "The Last Rose of Summer", the "Blue Bells of Scotland", "Auld Lang Syne" and "Home Sweet Home" were among the melodies sung. The show was later repeated for the general public with the profits going towards the organ fund. It drew a vast crowd and hundreds of disappointed people had to be turned away at the door. As a result the mayor announced that a further show would be given the following evening.

A total of £102 was raised for the organ fund, which already had accumulated over £1100.

The following Monday the juvenile members of the chorus were again in St. Andrew's Hall. This time the mayor was treating them all to a special tea as a reward for their labours. Seated at 3 long tables garnished with flowers, the youngsters consumed a substantial amount of food supplied by Mr. Pike after which they were entertained by a marionette display from the orchestra. The party lasted 3½ hours.

Other events took place to raise funds, one of which was a recital on 28th May 1880 given by Dr. Edward Bunnett on the new Willis organ in Prince's Street Congregational Church. It raised £9-13s-3d.

Byrceson Bros. submitted their organ specification to the committee. A special sub committee of Horace Hill, Dr. Bunnett, Dr. Gladstone, James Harcourt and C. E. Noverre, went through the builders' proposal, stop by stop. Several alterations and additions were made before a final specification of 33 stops was presented to the full committee in July. This was subsequently approved by themselves and Bryceson.

The organ case was still under consideration. Mr. Boardman suggested utilising the existing one. His idea was favourably received and he drew up a design to be made in oak using the old case for the central section with the addition of wings and overhang. The case design proposed by Bryceson Bros. was of pine and at a cost of £190 was also more expensive. Consequently Boardman's case was accepted.

An Italian church in Hatton Gardens, London expressed an interest in the old organ but when they withdrew, an offer of £100 from Bryceson was accepted.

By July 1880 the organ fund was only £250 short of its target.

To help to raise this sum Hugh Barclay, Geoffrey Buxton and Howard Taylor offered to open their 14 acres of woods and pleasure gardens to the public on 19th August 1880 between the hours of 2pm and dusk. Their properties Sunny Hill, Belle Vue and Pine Banks all nestled on a wooded slope approach by a lane opposite Thorpe Old Hall. Pine Banks, designed by architect E. Oldham Chambers of Lowestoft, was still being completed. It commanded an enviable position at the summit of the hill overlooking the Yare valley. On the brow had been built a tower, designed by the same architects. For a small additional charge, Taylor allowed people to climb the stone spiral stair case through the 5 floors to see one of the finest views in the country. On a clear day, with a good glass, one could see ships at Southwold and trace them along the sea line to Lowestoft and Yarmouth. To the north trains were visible leaving Cromer station.

The days preceding the garden party were dull and misty but on the morning of the 19th the sun put it a brief appearance. It was enough to entice 100's of people to take advantage of Great Eastern railway's offer of a return ticket for a single fare on their Cromer, Aylsham, Yarmouth and Lowestoft lines to Whitlingham or Norwich. The Norwich Omnibus Co. gallantly laid on a special service from the market place, their vehicles proving quite inadequate for the demand as by 2 o'clock the eastward route out of the city was a continuous stream of conveyances of all descriptions. A more leisurely route by way of the river was preferred by others.

Three commodious marquees had been erected in different parts of the grounds each offering an array of refreshments supplied by Mr. Cooper of Bank Plain. The Inniskilling Dragoon Band played on the side lawn of "Sunny Hill" under the direction of Mr. Webber. On the Pine Banks plateau Herr Dorla conducted the band of the Norfolk Artillery and on the lawn of Belle Vue the Orpheus quartet provided delightful vocal music.

Thousands of visitors, paying an admission of 1/-, wandered through this paradise of natural beauty. 210 people in groups of 12, ascended the 80 feet of Taylor's tower, passing through the gentlemen's room, studies, ladies room, smoking room and observatory, to the octagonal look out turret. The magnificent views were however shrouded by a vale of mist.

The public also had access to Mr. P. E Hansell's pretty garden at Holly Lodge situated at the foot of the hill where he obligingly allowed several parties to engage in tennis.

At 5 o'clock it began to drizzle but 4000 people had enjoyed a memorable day and raised £143 for the organ fund.

All through these fund raising activities, meetings and negotiations, Horace continued to give his services to musical concerts throughout the county.

The North Walsham Amateur Musical Society gave a performance of Rossini's "Stabat Mater" in January 1880. In March 1880, Mr. Mapleson, lessee of Her Majesty's Theatre, revisited the county with a party of his leading vocalists. On a Tuesday evening they gave a concert in the Music Hall at Lynn attracting a large and fashionable audience. The voices of Ilma de Murska, Mlle. Darialli, Mde. Marie Roze, Sig. Leli, Sig. Susini and Mr. Carleton were accompanied on the piano by Professor Hill. The hearty applause which followed each item resulted in many encores. There was also the added attraction of harpist Mlle. Sacconi whose solo playing provided a pleasing variation to the vocal programme.

The following evening the party repeated their performance in St. Andrew's Hall. Horace Hill provided the accompaniment.

In April, Horace was in the Girls' School Room, Cromer to accompany a concert on behalf of the Cromer Working Men's Reading Room. Mr. F. B. Noverre also made the journey. His playing of Scotch airs on the violin, accompanied by Horace on the piano, delighted the audience, their calls for an encore receiving a favourable response. At the close of the concert a vote of thanks was given to Horace Hill and F. B. Noverre for their gratuitous service.

A week later Horace was in Diss for a choral society concert in the Corn Hall. The programme commenced with an overture based on the hymn tune "St. Anne" which he had composed for the society 2 years earlier. During the evening Horace showed his ability as a bassoon player in a Reissiger trio with Mrs. H. Hill playing the piano and Mr. Bell, clarionet.

A concert given in early summer by the Norwich Philharmonic again found Horace playing the bassoon, this time in Beethoven's Septet with F. B. Noverre, violin; Henry Thouless, viola; Mr. Burton jun. violoncello; James Mottram, double bass; Francis Bell, clarionet and Mr. Charles Widdows, horn. The concert was conducted by James Harcourt. His son J. Arthur Harcourt being the accompanist.

138

James Harcourt's health was failing and in July, when the organ fund was approaching its target, he tendered his resignation as festival chorus master. In recognition of his past service he was awarded a year's salary. The resulting vacancy was advertised in the local newspapers on the 10th August 1880 and as the pleasurable activities of the Thorpe garden party filled the minds of many, Horace applied for the vacant post. He was the sole applicant and on 4th September 1880 it was announced that Dr. Horace Hill had been elected to follow in the footsteps of his father John and brother James Frederick, as the chorus master of the Norfolk and Norwich Triennial Festival.

CHAPTER 31

The Dream Comes True

Sir Julius Benedict had married for the second time in December 1879. He was in his 76th year; his bride Mary Fortey was a mere 22 years of age. The festival committee feared he would not be fit enough to carry out his duties at the next festival and decided the position would be more suited to a younger man. Chairman, Hay Gurney had the onerous task of breaking the news to Benedict. Arthur Sullivan and Alberto Randegger were both considered as possible replacements but when Sullivan requested a fee double that awarded to Sir Julius, the appointment went to Randegger.

A concert to mark Benedict's retirement was given in St. Andrew's Hall on Monday 18th October 1880 under the management of Messrs. Howlett. The hall was full. With admission charges ranging between 1/- to 6/- few could resist the temptation to see the youthful Lady Benedict. The newly weds received a rapturous reception which was similarly repeated for Alberto Randegger. The 2 gentlemen demonstrated their cordiality by playing a duet and Lady Benedict showed her pianistic talents by playing Chopin's Scherzo No 1 in B minor.

On the following Friday, subscribers to the organ fund attended a soirée in St. Andrew's Hall. They had been invited by the mayor, to witness the formal presentation of the new organ to the corporation. The mayor and lady mayoress welcomed their guests in the south porch, illuminated by Chinese lanterns for the occasion. The interior of the hall had been decorated by Charles Holborn to resembled a drawing room. An expanse of crimson cloth covered the floor and the orchestra, upon which potted palms and shrubs were elegantly grouped. Cocoa nut matting paved the side aisles. The walls, hung with scarlet fabric inset with gold coloured panelling, displayed banners bearing appropriate mottoes such as "Difficulties Delight the Brave". Scarlet fabric also swathed the bases of the pillars and flags drooped from the capitals. A refreshment buffet extended along the north aisle supervised by Mr. Marston of the Walk and at the west end a dark cretonne screen shielded the cloak room from view.

At 8 o'clock Hugh Barclay, the organ fund treasurer led Dr. Horace Hill, and other members of the organ fund committee to their places on the south side of the orchestral platform. On the

Alberto Randegger

north side a large body of corporation officials assembled. Cheers resounded around the hall as the mayor Harry Bullard; the sheriff, Mr. P. Back and the deputy mayor, Mr. J. D Smith took up their positions.

Hugh Barclay opened the proceedings by sketching the events of the past few months. In under a year £1841-8s-0d had been raised. The cost of the new instrument totalled £1875-8s-5d. Instantly the short fall was erased by Mr. Gorell who generously donated a cheque for £35. Barclay paid tribute to the fund's 3 secretaries, Walter Hansell, Charles Noverre and William Heaver whose patience, tact and indefatigable energy had resulted in the erection of this organ for the enjoyment of the city. He then presented the instrument to Mayor Bullard saying "I beg to present you with this organ which I trust you will accept on behalf of the Corporation ..... I know it will be properly cared for by you and your colleagues in the council ...and that you ..... will always endeavour to keep it for the pleasure, instruction and recreation of our fellow citizens........" His speech was frequently interrupted by cheers and applause from the audience and at its conclusion, a further cheer went up as the curtain before the organ was gradually lowered, revealing a bright new instrument with tastefully ornamented front pipes.

The mayor, in his reply, stated how it was only right that "those who had subscribed to the fund should be the first to welcome its opening".

With the formalities over Dr. Frederick Bridge, organist of Westminster Abbey, played the National Anthem after which a composite recital progressed as follows:-

Fantasia and Fugue (C minor) . . . . .Gustav Merkel
Andante and variations . . . . .Lemmens
March and Chorus ("Ruins of Athens") . . . . . .Beethoven
DR. BRIDGE
Andante and Allegro Fuga from
Organ Concerto . . . . .Crotch
DR. BUNNETT
Introduction and air with variations . . . . .Hesse
DR. GLADSTONE
Pilgrims' Chorus (Tannhäuser) arranged by
Liszt . . . . .Wagner
DR. BRIDGE
An interval of half an hour

Frederick Bridge

Ave Maria (by request) . . . . .Bunnett
DR. BUNNETT
Air from the Water Music and Allegro from the Cuckoo
and Nightingale Concerto . . . . .Handel
DR. GLADSTONE
Prelude and Fugue (B Minor) . . . . .Bach
DR. BRIDGE
Fantasia für die Orgel .Berens
DR. BUNNETT
Festive March . . . . .H Smart
DR. GLADSTONE
Allegretto . . . . .Gade
Marches des Templiers (Arranged for
the organ by J F Bridge . . . . .Sir J Benedict
DR. BRIDGE

All through the recital the audience chatted constantly. On 3 occasions the mayor had to ask for silence so music lovers could actually hear the instrument.

The following evening Dr. Bunnett, in his capacity of the newly appointed corporation organist, gave a public recital. There was not a large attendance.

The sense of triumph which lingered after this monumental achievement was dashed on 22nd November 1880 when news circulated of the tragic death of Mr. Henry Jonathan Minns at the age of 34. Mr. Minns, a lay clerk of the cathedral, had frequently participated in Horace's concerts and performed duets with his daughter, Bessie. This fine tenor left Norwich on 30th September for a holiday. After 3 weeks he had not returned and was found in London in a poor state of physical and mental health. Minns was brought back to Norwich and on 20th October was attended by surgeon, Charles Williams who found him confined to his bed depressed in mind and feeble in body. As the excitement of the new organ surrounded other musicians, Minns laid in this wretched condition, being revisited by the surgeon on the 28th who diagnosed melancholia. At half past eleven on the morning of Monday 22nd November 1880, a meeting took place at the cathedral during which Dr. Bensley sent his clerk, Byron Foreman on an errand to the presbytery triforium over St. Lukes Chapel. As Foreman made his way back, in the dullness of light, he noticed a ladder. For a moment he assumed a workman was engaged about some business but then recognised the features of Mr. Minns. He hastily reported his findings. The sub sacrist, Mr. Alden, and a carpenter returned to the scene. Minns was found with his back upon the rungs of the ladder, around his neck was a piece of cord; the end of which had been fastened to one of the upper staves. His body was cold.

Mr. Henry Jonathan Minns was interred in the grave of Samuel William Minns aged 64 years* who had died on the same day 3 years previous. The headstone bears the inscription "Henry J. Minns, for many years lay clerk of the cathedral"... "In the midst of life we are in death"

*Grave of Samuel William Minns, Section H 1264, Rosary Cemetery.

CHAPTER 32

The R.A.M. comes to Norwich

The dawn light of the 12th January 1881 revealed a city under 6 inches of snow. Over the next 2 weeks citizens endured arctic conditions as temperatures plummeted to 23 degrees of frost. The river Yare froze and navigation was brought to a halt. On the 18th a ferocious gale buffeted the east coast for 24 hours, such strength of wind had rarely been experienced. At 5 o'clock that afternoon, thick snow began to fall and drifts 10 feet deep accumulated. Rail travel was suspended. The city's streets became deserted as people remained indoors.

These atrocious conditions led to the postponement of a complimentary concert to James Harcourt scheduled for the 28th January. The conditions however did not deter Horace Hill and Edward Bunnett from travelling to Diss on the 20th January for a choral society concert. Other performers journeyed from Ipswich, Lynn, East Winch, Narborough and Norwich to take part. Despite the bad weather the concert attracted a goodly attendance. The miscellaneous programme commenced with Bunnett's setting of the 130th psalm which was capitally rendered by all concerned; Mr. H. J. Brookes, the newly appointed cathedral lay clerk, taking the tenor part. At its conclusion loud continuous applause coaxed Bunnett on to the platform to bow his acknowledgements. His psalm setting was followed by a selection from Haydn's "Creation" conducted by Horace Hill.

James Harcourt's Complimentary Concert to mark his retirement from musical life eventually took place in mid February, under the management of Messrs. Darken and Son. There was little improvement in the weather, consequently this somewhat limited the attendance. Horace commenced the programme by conducting Pierson's "Ye Mariners". Dr. Gladstone had originally offered his services as accompanist but his resignation as cathedral organist in January meant he had since left the city. Edward Bunnett kindly took over his part and with Arthur Bunnett, Arthur Harcourt and Kingston Rudd performed a piano quartet by Benedict. Vocalist, Miss May Bell, who for the past 6 weeks had been suffering with congestion of the lungs, was determined not to break her promise to sing. Her delightful soprano voice showed no signs of imperfection and she soon won the hearts of the audience. The violinist Herr Richard Gompertz, a pupil of Joachim, inspired an enthusiastic response with his superb unaccompanied playing of a Bach Allemande and Fugue in G mnr, and obligingly provided an encore.

Unfortunately the concert failed in its financial aim through lack of support.

The Royal Academy of Music established Norwich as one of its local examination centres for independent students in February 1881. Dr. Horace Hill was appointed Local Examiner. All applications of entry being sent to his St. Stephen's Gate residence by 1st March 1881. This family home now had the addition of Ernest, Gilbert, Eliza and Mildred (15). The birth of their last child Frank Wilson Hill was awaited (18). 26 candidates put themselves forward for examination in the following subjects; I Counterpoint, harmony and plan or design, II Singing, III Pianoforte and IV Playing orchestral instruments. Examinations were held on Tuesday 22nd March, conducted by Mr. F. W. Davenport of the Academy staff who was the son in law of the principal Prof. Macfarren, and Dr. Horace Hill. The results, announced in early May showed Mr. Flowers, organ; Miss Katie Shaw, piano; Miss Nellie Rix, piano and Mr F. W. B. Noverre, violin; had all gained honours, each receiving a certificate signed by the Principal.

On Friday 10th June 1881 Horace attended the funeral of Mr. William Howlett at the Rosary cemetery. His friend and fellow musician had died on 31st May at his Thorpe home after a short illness. Howlett had been a Town Councillor in the 4th ward, a governor of the Jenny Lind Infirmary and a member of the sub committee of the music festival. Standing among the large crowd of mourners at the grave side with Horace were James Mottram, C. E Noverre, E. Boardman, Dr. Bunnett, J. Darken, Walter Lain and Byron Foreman. The service was conducted by the Rev. George Follows minister of the Wesleyan Chapel, Lady's Lane where the deceased had worshipped and the Rev. J. J. J. Kempter. The latter paid tribute to Howlett, a genial hearted gentleman, who had used his musical talents to raise much money for local charities. In his last week of life he had been promoting festivities for the workhouse inmates to mark the Queen's birthday.

With the kind and benevolent acts of this gentleman at the forefront of their minds, the mourners watched the polished oak coffin with brass fittings, descend into the large family grave*.

* The Howlett family grave is marked by an urn mounted on a pedestal. Section F1/900. Rosary cemetery.

CHAPTER 33

Randegger, the Festival Conductor

A new age was dawning in the city. During August 1881 2 electric standard lamps were erected in the Market Place. They proved so successful that soon all the main thoroughfares were similarly illuminated.

Horace and his chorus attended rehearsals for the coming festival every Monday, Wednesday and Friday evening in St. Andrew's Hall. From the outset their new chorus master made it quite clear he would not tolerate irregular attendance. The main cause of his annoyance being the behaviour of some of the tenors. Their conduct was so bad Horace suggested to the festival committee that if no improvement occurred, steps would need to be taken to replace them with selected voices from the Hallé chorus. This did not become necessary.

Just 2 months before the festival Benedict withdrew his new cantata "Griziella" which he was composing expressly for the occasion. He disapproved of the work being placed in the Friday evening concert. The composition was still far from completion and the limited time left for rehearsals would have been insufficient.

An orchestral suite, promised by E. D'Albert also did not materialise, owing to the composer's ill health.

When the festival visitors approached St. Andrew's Hall on the evening of Tuesday 11th October 1881, they found the Plain bathed in the beams from a swan electric light by Crompton & Co. The mayor, sheriff, members of the corporation and their families were present in the audience as Bessie Hill and Mrs. H. Hill took their places in the soprano and contralto sections of the chorus. Mr. J. T. Carrodus led the band and after an arrangement of the National Anthem by Costa, Mendelssohn's oratorio, "St. Paul" commenced. The work was sung with precision and accuracy of the highest degree. A fine reward for the chorus master who had brought them to the pitch of perfection. The work received a much more favourable response than in 1864 under James Frederick. Wednesday morning's concert opened with Schubert's "Unfinished" symphony. Those who arrived late found the doors of the hall closed at the request of the new festival conductor, Randegger. No one was allowed to enter whilst a performance was in progress. Too often in the past performances had been disrupted

Arthur Sullivan

by this kind of intrusion. After the symphony Horace received a gratifying reception as he took up the baton to conduct a motett, attributed to a member of the Bach family, for double chorus and quartet; the quartet being sung by Mrs. Osgood, Mde. Mudie - Bolingbroke, Mr. Barton McGuckin and Mr. Brockbank (of the cathedral choir). A concerto in E minor for organ and orchestra by Ebenezer Prout followed giving Edward Bunnett the opportunity to display the quality of the new organ. However the work was said to be "caviar to the multitude" for it was not until the last 2 movements that the audience showed any appreciation of this "scholarly" work. At the commencement of the second part of the programme Arthur Sullivan, amidst loud applause took his seat to conduct his sacred music drama "The Martyr of Antioch". It was the first hearing of the work in Norwich. The chorus had been drilled exclusively by Horace and proved themselves to be most competent. At the close of this 4 act work the delight of the audience was testified by their repeated applause. Sullivan returned to the platform to acknowledge their approval.

Wednesday evening found a drop in attendance. Berlioz "Faust" was the main work, its complete title being deliberately curtailed because it was felt to be too profane. Even some of the chorus had shown a reluctance to take part. The final rehearsal on the Monday attracted 1100 people who paid an admission charge of 2/6d but only 897 came to hear the full performance.

Attendance revived on Thursday. Beethoven's "Egmont Overture" commenced the morning programme. Randegger then stepped aside so Frederic Cowen could conduct his sacred cantata "St Ursula" which he had composed expressly for the festival. The work was enthusiastically received and Cowen, having been recalled to the orchestra, recognised their approval. The second part of the concert featured Mendelssohn's "Athalie". Racine's dialogue being recited by Mr. Santley.

The news that Mde. Albani had consented to sing 2 additional songs in the evening miscellaneous concert brought a boost in ticket sales. Her singing of "Home Sweet Home" and "Ah Fors e Lui" from Verdi's "La Traviata" earned her an extra £52-10s-0d on top of her agreed fee of £472-10s-0d (16). This concert included a choral ode "The Sun Worshippers" by Goring Thomas, an overture "Henry V" by Walter Macfarren, a part song "The Better Land" by A. R. Gaul, conducted by the composer before it concluded with the March from Costa's "Eli".

Frederic Cowen

Friday was a very windy day with heavy showers. Trees were uprooted, roof tops damaged and one of the electric standards in the Market Place snapped. Even the west window of St. Andrew's Hall threatened to cave in through the force of the gale. But still every available space within was filled to hear the morning's performance of Handel's "Messiah".

The evening concert was also well attended. J. F. Barnett conducted his symphonic poem "Harvest Festival" which was based on a poem by Mary Lemon. The work, composed expressly for the festival, was cordially received with Barnett returning to the platform to accept the usual compliment. Eaton Faning conducted his spirited chorus "The Vikings". Mde. Patey sang Stephen Adams' song "The Children of the City" and the musical festivities concluded with the overture to Cherubini's "Ali Baba". Alberto Randegger, Edward Bunnett and Horace Hill were called forward to receive a deserved ovation.

That evening the chorus had shown signs of weariness. Altogether they had attended 80 rehearsals and the demand upon them had been greater than ever before. Horace received for his labours a total of £50 which included his rail fare to London for rehearsals in the capital; Randegger, £105 and Edward Bunnett, £25 (16).

The festival had 8188 visitors. Although the attendance was higher than in 1878, admission charges had been reduced to 15/- 10/- and 5/- for some concerts. However a handsome sum was still donated to charity. The Norfolk and Norwich Hospital received £200, the Jenny Lind Infirmary £50, the West Norfolk and Lynn Hospital £40, Yarmouth Hospital £40, the Norwich Dispensary £35, the Norwich Sick Poor Society £35, the Norwich District Visiting Society £35, the Eye Infirmary £30, the Lowestoft Convalescent Home £30, the Norwich Nurses Institute £25, the Norwich Lying-in charity £20, the Benevolent Fund for Decayed Tradesmen £10, the Stanley Home £10 and the Orphans Home £10. A donation to charity of £25 was also made by Mde. Albani (16).

Two weeks after the festival, Horace presided over a meeting of the Norwich Philharmonic Society held at the Castle Hotel. An excellent supper was served. He had recently been appointed conductor of the society following the resignation of James Harcourt. The meeting agreed to subscribe to a music library so that a wider variety of new and novel pieces could be tried at their practice sessions on alternate Saturday and Thursday evenings.

In the new year of 1882 the Society gave a concert in Noverre's room. The mayor and lady mayoress were among the numerous audience. Haydn's "Military" Symphony opened the programme followed by a violin concerto with string accompaniment by Rode, Sterndale Bennett's Fantasie-Overture "Paradise and Peri", Mozart's symphony No 4 in D and his quintet in A major for clarionet and strings. Songs by Handel, Spohr and Victor Masse added contrast to the programme which concluded with the overture to Nicolai's "Merry Wives of Windsor".

The R.A.M. examinations in Norwich took place on Thursday 16th March 1881. This time Horace was examining with Walter Fritton. The results later revealed that pianists Mary Ann Hobbins, Maud Mary Maddle and Fanny Faulkes had all gained honours. The next day a similar examination session was held in the Town Hall at Lynn, where 12 candidates had put themselves forward.

At the time of the examinations Horace and Edward Bunnett were preparing a performance of the "Messiah" for Good Friday afternoon, with some 250 local musicians. The Norwich Philharmonic Society, assisted by 2 lady violinists from Diss, formed the band comprising of 11 first violins, 12 second violins, 4 violas, 5 violoncello, 5 contra basso, 1 flute, 2 oboes, 2 clarionets, 4 bassoons, 2 horns, 2 trumpets, 3 trombones and drums under the leadership of F. W. B. Noverre. Miss Helen Stark soprano, Miss Bertha Alden contralto, Mr. Meers tenor and Mr. A. S. Kinnell baritone took the solo parts and members of the festival chorus completed the ensemble. On Good Friday, Great Eastern Railway offered a return ticket to Norwich for a single fare from all its stations. Admission to the performance was 1/- and by 3 o 'clock Good Friday afternoon St. Andrew's Hall was filled with over 2000 people. A specially printed message awaited, requesting them not to applaud. Their appreciation could therefore only be ascertained from the favourable departing comments.

The performance raised in excess of £100 for local charities; the time and talent of all concerned being freely given.

CHAPTER 34

R.C.M.

There was a growing school of thought in Britain who believed that music, when correctly taught, refined and elevated the mind. It purified emotions, satisfied natural cravings and provide a healthy alternative to drink. Even if indulged to excess, it produced no harmful side effects.

In 1882 the Royal College of Music was in the process of being formed by H. R. H. the Prince of Wales. The Prince had been President of the Norfolk and Norwich Music Festival since February 1881. The Mayor of Norwich and the Earl of Leicester both received a letter inviting the citizens of Norwich and inhabitants of Norfolk to support his project.

A public meeting was convened for Saturday 22nd April 1882 in St. Andrew's Hall commencing at half past one. Among the noblemen, gentlemen and musicians present were the Bishop of Norwich; Lord Suffield; the Mayor of Norwich, W. Hunter; the Sheriff of Norwich, J. J. Winter; the Mayor of Yarmouth, C.C. Aldred; J. J. Colman and family; James Mottram; William Heaver; Kingston Rudd; Edward Bunnett and Horace Hill. The situation was related to them and it was explained how the College would be equally accessible to the rich and the poor.

The mayor then moved "That the County of Norfolk and City of Norwich unite in giving support to the Royal College of Music now being formed under the presidency of the Prince of Wales..." Letters of support had already been received from those unable to attend and the resolution was unanimously adopted.

Comment was made on how English singers frequently took Italian names in an attempt to disguise their nationality. It was hoped the new college would eliminate the need for this practice. The college required between £10,000 and £12,000 to achieve its objectives. At the suggestion of Sir R. J. Buxton, a subscription list was set up and before the company departed over £1500 had been pledged. The largest sum, £500, being donated by J. J. Colman. These people of Norfolk and Norwich had set an example which it was hoped other regions would follow, their generosity helping to provide for future generations of musicians.

Their generous donations however discouraged small contributions and an appeal was launched for 1 guinea subscriptions. Popular concerts were also given in aid of the fund with little profit being made, but by October the fund had swelled to £2687-3s-6d.

The Brinsmead concert company of Preston under the management of Mr. William Benson was travelling the country raising funds for the college, with favourable results. Mr. Howlett engaged the company to appear in Norwich on 30th November 1882. The company under the conductorship of Sig. Bisaccia, had the attractions of soloists Miss Anna Williams, Mde. Patey, Sig. Runcio and Sig. Foli; the pianist Chevalier de Kontski and violinist Herr Poznanski. The concert was musically a success but added nothing to the fund.

Although the concerts in aid of the R.C.M. fund were on the whole monetary failures other concerts in the city succeeded in their aim. The English Opera Company, during their week at the theatre, agreed to give a concert in St. Andrew's Hall on the morning of 1st June 1882 in aid of the Jenny Lind Infirmary. The troupe had the able assistance of the festival chorus and the Norwich Philharmonic Society. Benedict volunteered to conduct as he would be in Norwich that day to conduct an evening performance of "The Lily of Killarney". When the audience began to arrive so did the news that Benedict had missed his train. At a moments notice Horace undertook the conducting of the first part of the concert, Rossini's "Stabat Mater", proving himself to be a thorough master of the art. Benedict arrived for the commencement of the second part receiving an enthusiastic ovation from the audience.

On the evening of Friday 6th October 1882 Horace travelled to Great Ryburgh to conducted the first concert of the Great Ryburgh Amateur Musical Society. A miscellaneous programme of choruses, duets, songs and instrumental trios was pleasingly performed. Miss Buller, Miss Saxton, Mr. C. Tatham and Mr. W. Tatham, being justly praise for their renderings of the various vocal items.

Mendelssohn's popular oratorio "Elijah" was performed in St. Andrew's Hall on December 14th by the Norwich Festival chorus creditably assisted by the Norwich Philharmonic band and admirably conducted by Horace. The solo parts were entrusted to Miss Robertson, soprano; Annie Butterworth, contralto; Hirwen Jones, tenor and Lucas Williams, bass. Annie had taken the place of Miss Fanny Robertson who was indisposed; her performance met with approval from the audience. Mr. Jones showed himself worthy of such good company and Mr. Williams' rendering of the arduous part of the prophet was satisfactorily executed. They were joined by Bessie Hill, Miss Alden, Mr. A. H. Alden and Mr. R. J. Mallett in "For He Shall Give His Angels".

Horace had devoted much time and effort in the preparing the concert. His performers repaid him handsomely.

CHAPTER 35

Guilmant plays in St. Andrew's Hall

Horace began the new year of 1883 by conducting a North Walsham Amateur Musical Society concert in the National School room. During the miscellaneous first part, Mr. Barker of London played "Autumn" by J. Thomas upon the harp. Sullivan's "The Martyr of Antioch" formed the second part; Horace being congratulated on a the most successful rendering of this "difficult" work.

Messrs. Howlett and Son began the year by announcing that M. Alexandre Guilmant, organist of La Trinité, of the Societé des concerts du conservatoire and of the Palace of the Trocadéro, Paris, was to give 2 organ recitals in St Andrew's Hall on Tuesday 6th February. Admission charges were either 2/-, 1/- or 6d. The visit had been planned for the previous December but was postponed. It was thought the recitals would be of special interest to village organists so, to encourage their attendance, people travelling from outside a 5 mile radius of the city were allowed to purchase reserved seats at half price; their rail ticket providing proof of distance.

Guilmant opened the 3 o'clock recital with Handel's 10th organ concerto in D mnr. As he began the allegro movement the bellows failed. The supply of water to the hydraulic power was speedily increased and this unfortunate experience did not reoccur. The virtuoso's masterly technique then flowed unhindered through Bach's Fuga in G mnr, Lemmens' Prayer in F and his own Sonata in D. A most astonishing improvisation on the theme "Those Evening Bells" selected by the Rev. William Vincent on behalf of the audience was however the highlight of the recital.

In the evening Bach's D mnr Toccata and Fuga, Mendelssohn's 6th Sonata in D mnr, and a Caprice in B♭ by the presiding organist, were all expertly played. The improvised theme on this occasion, "Rule Britannia", was selected by the lady mayoress. The tune, in various guises, was clearly recognisable throughout, much to the delight of his listeners. At the close, the vast audience rose and heartily demonstrated their appreciation as Guilmant descended from his seat at the organ. He gracefully acknowledged their compliment.

As Easter approached Horace drilled the North Walsham Amateur Musical Society for a performance of Macfarren's

"Outward Bound". He was also busy in Norwich preparing another Good Friday "Messiah" with Edward Bunnett. St Andrew's Hall was full to the extreme for this popular oratorio, the rows of chairs being placed uncomfortably close and all available standing room, taken. A handsome sum was again raised for local charities. The Good Friday "Messiah" became a regular event in the city's musical calendar.

On the afternoon of Monday 7th May the Royal College of Music at Kensington Gore was officially opened; the ceremony taking place on the second floor of the building.

1588 applicants had contested for 50 scholarships. In March local assessment centres, one of which was at Norwich trimmed the entries down to 480. During April every one of these remaining candidates was examined either at the College or at the Albert Hall reducing the total to 76. The final 50 were selected in a conclave assembly by the professors of the college with 17 piano, 13 singing, 8 violin, 6 composition, 2 violoncello, 1 organ, 1 flute, 1 harp and 1 clarionet student being selected. The daughter of a brick maker, the son of a farm labourer and a mill girl were among them. Not one came from Norfolk.

The city's musical tradition however, continued to flourish. The Norwich Philharmonic gave their 65th concert at the end of May with Horace conducting an excellent programme of music. Commencing with the 7th of Haydn's Salomon symphonies, the audience then heard the overture "Ruy Blas" by Mendelssohn and contrasting dances from the works of Rameau and Sullivan. Mr. R. Price contributed a cello solo and Kingston Rudd played 2 movements from a piano concerto by Hummel. Miss Josephine Pulham of the R.A.M. added further variety to the programme by charmingly singing "Trust Not", a recently written song by Horace.

The concert was tinged with sadness as James Harcourt had died just a few days previous. For 30 years he had been conductor of the society until ill health forced his retirement in 1880. From then on he was granted honorary membership of the society as a mark of respect.

Over the summer months Horace Hill, Edward Bunnett, Kingston Rudd and James Arthur Harcourt prepared the musical activities for the grand opening of the new Norfolk and Norwich hospital on 20th August. At 2pm a train carrying the Duke and Duchess of Connaught steamed into Thorpe station having left

South Willingham at 10.30 that morning. It was exactly on time. The station had been decorated for the occasion. Scarlet cloth panelled with evergreens draped the walls of the platform. The mayor, C. R. Gilman; the sheriff S. Newman; the deputy mayor, W. Hunter, the Earl of Leicester and hospital representatives, greeted the Royal party. 5 awaiting carriages conveyed them to the hospital by way of Prince of Wales Rd, Bank Plain, London St, the Market Place, Rampant Horse St. and St. Stephen's St. 1000's of people lined the route which had been gaily decorated. The vinegar factory in Prince of Wales Rd. provided one of the prettiest sights with venetian masts of mauve and white carrying festoons of evergreen studded with artificial flowers. Above the gate was an illuminated "crown" surmounted with a trophy of flags and over the workmen's entrance was a pink tablet bearing the word "Welcome".

At the corner of London St. and the Walk, Howlett's Music Warehouse presented a pleasing appearance. Every few yards flags hung from the scarlet covered balcony. Each window was emblazoned with shields, emblems and crests. Over the entrance was the Royal coat of arms. A cheering crowd heralded the procession's approach to the hospital and as the carriages drew into the hospital yard the band of the 7th Hussars played the National Anthem. Prince Albert Victor had arrived earlier that day with his host Edward Birkbeck of Horstead Hall and joined the party for luncheon prior to the opening ceremony.

A little after 3 o'clock the ceremony began. The nurses in their "neat costumes" were stationed on a platform with the cathedral choir, dressed in purple cassocks. Under the command of Mr. Brockbank, the hymn "O Lord of Heaven, Earth and Sea" was sung softly accompanied by a military band. Prayers followed.

Once the ceremony had been completed a Grand Bazaar was declared open. Over the next 5 days exhibitions of fine arts were on view in the 2 large wards of the new hospital wing overlooking the public road and in the grounds, with legerdemain, magic lantern shows, music and drama to entertain.

Having toured the various hospital departments the Royal party left the city by way of Chapelfield Rd., St. Giles' St., London St., Queen St., Tombland, Wensum St. and Magdalen St. for Catton Hall where they were the guests of S. Gurney Buxton esq.

In the evening Horace conducted a Grand Concert in St. Andrew's Hall; Edward Bunnett commencing this miscellaneous programme with an organ solo. A selection of instrumental, violin, violoncello and piano pieces were intermixed with choruses and solo songs by Bessie Hill before "Be Not Afraid" from "Elijah" drew the concert to a close.

The next morning the Royal visitors attended the cathedral before leaving for London at 2.55pm.

The excitement had hardly subsided when the death was announced of Alfred Master F.R.C.S. On September 3rd this medical gentleman who had cared for Horace's brother, James Frederick, passed away aged 67 years. A large number of professional and social friends gathered at St. Giles' church for the first part of the funeral service conducted by the Rev. W. Ripley. The plain polished oak coffin of the deceased, almost hidden by the volume of floral tributes, rested on a bier at the west end of the church. As the coffin was transferred to the hearse, Horace played a solemn voluntary. The cortège then proceeded to the Earlham cemetery* for the remainder of the service.

In the autumn Spohr's little heard oratorio "The Fall of Babylon" was performed by the festival chorus, under the skilful direction of Horace Hill. The Norwich Philharmonic was reinforced for the occasion and their interpretation of the "difficult" orchestration was beyond all expectations. Horace again received high praise for the standards achieved.

As the year of 1883 drew to a close Guilmant returned to St. Andrew's Hall to give 2 further organ recitals. Both were well supported. More of his own compositions were heard along with those of J. S. Bach, Handel, Dr. Wesley, Berlioz and Liszt. His improvisations, this time on "Ein' Feste Burg" and "Home Sweet Home" again amazed and delighted the audiences.

Alfred Master's grave is situated in Section 6 No 169.

CHAPTER 36

The Prince's visit of 1884

At the beginning of February 1884 Horace conducted the inaugural concert of the South Heigham Musical Society. A performance of "Acis and Galatea" and a miscellaneous selection of pieces were given in the Parochial Hall with Mrs. Marriott, the Rev. E. J. Alvis, Mr. J. Lincoln and Mr. A. R. Hart assisting with the production. The same month Horace conducted a Norwich Philharmonic concert. Their excellent programme included Mozart's "Jupiter" Symphony, Cherubini's overture to "Anacreon" and harp solos by Miss Trust.

Mid April found members of the North Walsham Amateur Musical Society assisting with an evening of recitations from Shakespeare's Macbeth read by Samuel Brandram. Appropriate miscellaneous musical items were conducted by Horace. The singers, Miss Hadley, Mrs. John Wilkinson and the Rev. W. Farley Wilkinson were accompanied on the harmonium by John Dixon, ably assisted on the piano by Master Hill.

By Easter news had reached the city of Sir Michael Costa's "dangerous" state of health. Through his connections with the Norfolk and Norwich festival he was well known and respected by many. Costa died on 29th April 1884 at his residence in Seafield Villas, West Brighton. He was buried in Kensal Green cemetery, his funeral being attended by many musicians and representatives from musical societies.

The Norwich Philharmonic gave another concert on 28th May. Horace conducted Tulou's 13th grand flute concerto as well as works by the great masters. A week later South Heigham Musical Society gave their second concert. This time Horace was directing a performance of Benedict's "Undine"; his daughter Bessie taking the soprano part.

As the summer progressed an abominable smell spread over the city. It plagued the area between the Market Place and Mousehold at various times both day and night. People became increasingly concerned for their health as it caused a feeling of nausea and general discomfort. The District Medical Officer tried to allay fears by stating that bad smells seldom proved to be prejudicial to health. But by the nature of the odour and the direction from whence it came, little doubt was left in peoples' minds that the smell originated from the gas works in St. Martin at Palace. An inspection of the site was carried out. No fault was found and the problem subsided.

Horace was busy rehearsing for the next festival. The Prince and Princess of Wales had expressed a desire to attend. Mackenzie had written an oratorio "The Rose of Sharon" and Stanford a choral "Elegiac Ode" especially for the occasion. Horace's part song "The Calm" was also to be performed.

The festival committee engaged the opera singer Miss Emma Nevada as the leading soloist for a fee of £315 (17). The lady, who had taken her name from her place of birth, Nevada City, California, was very popular in Europe.

Alberto Randegger was again to conduct. On Whit Monday he had married his pupil Fräulein Adeline Maria Elizabeth De Leuw, at St. Paul's Church, Avenue Rd., Regent's Park.

A general meeting of the festival committee took place on 6th September in the Guildhall. After its conclusion Mr. J. J.Winter addressed those assembled. He reminded those present of the £2650 subscribed to the R.C.M., stating how regrettable it was that £3000 had not been raised to enable Norfolk to secure a scholarship in its own name. Even Sir George Grove, the director of the College, had remarked what a pity it was that such an important county as Norfolk was without a scholarship. Winter persuaded the meeting that the sum already collected would prove more valuable to the local community should the shortfall be found. If achieved by the Wednesday morning of the festival, the money could be presented to the Prince of Wales in person. Immediately an appeal for 1 guinea subscriptions was launched. Two lists were commenced, one for gentlemen: the other for ladies, headed by Mr. and Mrs. Eade, the mayor and lady mayoress. In just one week 40 donations had been received.

However by the beginning of October £200 was still required. Time was running short. People were encouraged to give by reminding them of how their generosity could provide a local talented child from the poorest of families with free tuition, education and board should the remainder of the money for a scholarship be forthcoming.

On the day before the festival £55 was still needed but Winter had every confidence the target would be reached.

This Monday morning found Randegger and Mackenzie attending the final rehearsal of the "Rose of Sharon". Afterwards Horace and the choir retired to the Victoria Hall* in St. Andrew's

Broad Street for dinner provided and served by Mr. Snelling. As hearty toasts were being raised to the Queen and the Prince of Wales, Randegger and Mackenzie arrived being greeted with enthusiastic cheering. The chairman P. E. Hansell then called on Mr. Ladell to make a presentation to Dr. Horace Hill, the festival chorus master.

Over the past few years Horace had worked earnestly to bring the choir to a state of perfection. Of late his work had been both hard and laborious having the great responsibility of training the chorus in "The Rose of Sharon", a "difficult" work, but they had triumphed. To show their appreciation the chorus made a collection amongst themselves. Horace graciously received their gift of a writing table, a chair, a lamp, an inkstand and a volume containing a list of subscribers in recognition of his valuable service. Further toasts were drunk and "For He's a Hearty Good Fellow" was sung with a freedom which would have been totally unacceptable at a festival performance.

Outside barriers were being erected along the streets, to hold back the expectant crowds whilst porticos were under construction in St. George's St. and St. Andrew's Plain to provide protection against the elements. Inside, the hall was being transformed in the usual manner and the Royal suite was being prepared.

On the Tuesday evening festival visitors arrived early for the performance of "Elijah" and were all seated by the time the principal guests took their places on the platform. There was confusion as to whether applause during the performance was permitted so only a slight demonstration of appreciation was shown. Miss Nevada's performance showed signs of nervousness and did little to justify her popularity. She had little experience of singing oratorio.

The next morning the Prince and Princess arrived at the City station at 11.40am. They had journeyed from King's Cross to Peterborough on Monday and thence by special train to Melton Constable being met at the station by Lord Hastings, their host, at 5.15pm. On this Wednesday morning the Royal party was met by civic dignitaries. Flags flew from the 2 towers of the brightly decorated station as the procession, escorted by a detachment of the 4th Hussars, emerged to a cheering crowd. It proceeded along Barn Rd. where French pennants on either side gave colour to the street and also hid some unsightly cottages from view. After proceeding along Dereham Rd for a short distant, where spruce

A. C. Mackenzie

trees in tubs lined the road, they entered Distillery St. The cortège was faced with a blaze of colour. From every house flags and banners hung in abundance. Turning into St. Giles the crowds thickened. The scaffolding poles surrounding the partly constructed Catholic church displayed a variety of decorations. Nearer to the city, the Norfolk Hotel draped a purple valance edged with a deep orange fringe from the mouldings of its first floor windows. A similar decoration adorned the windows of the second floor. At the end of the street a throng of people watched the procession turn into Exchange St., cheering enthusiastically in the misty rain. On the corner, the frontage of Messrs. Jarrold shop had been swathed in light blue and ecru cloth gathered in pleats to form alternate perpendicular stripes, each adorned with ornamental shields. Barriers then kept the crowds at bay to St. Andrew's Hall. This circular route had been chosen to avoid the awkward turning at the Three Pigeons public house in Upper Westwick St.

Inside the hall the first performance in Norwich of Gounod's sacred trilogy "The Redemption" had commenced. The prologue having just been completed as the Royal couple entered the hall accompanied by the mayor. The music came to a halt as the audience rose to their feet and remained standing until the party was seated. Copies of the words were handed to the Prince and Princess by Mr. P. E. Hansell. That for the Princess being bound in white morocco with gilt edging; an elegant gold pattern adorning the side. The Prince's copy bore the same design but was bound in scarlet morocco. The binding of these handsome souvenirs had been carried out by Messrs. Fletcher and Son. A 40 minute interval was taken for lunch. The Prince and Princess were escorted by way of the crypt to their specially prepared suite of rooms, comprising of a general reception room, two dressing rooms, a smoking room and a ladies boudoir; all lavishly decorated and furnished. The walls of the Royal luncheon room were covered 12 feet high with pale blue and ecru pleated satennes. Below, a dado of peacock blue 2 feet 6 inches high, panelled with palm leaves was topped by a frieze of deep blue festooned with gold tassels. The ceiling was cover white, striped with crimson cloth, the latter also covered the floor.

A sumptuous menu of clear turtle soup, Julienne soup, sweetbreads, cutlets aux champignons, swan, woodcock, snipe, boned turkey, roast pheasant, roast partridge, raised pigeon pie, pâté de foie gras, tongue, lobster salad and oyster patties, awaited. For dessert, meringues, vanilla cream, raspberry cream, jelly, grapes, peaches, pines and Neapolitan ices tempted the palate.

During the oratorio the Earl of Leicester had informed the Prince of J. J. Winter's successful appeal to fund a Norfolk Scholarship. After the concert Winter was summoned to the Royal apartments where the Prince shook his hand and expressed his great pleasure at the result of his labours. The Prince and Princess then left the hall for the Norfolk and Norwich hospital by way of Redwell St. and London St. During the past weeks the shop fronts en route had been freshly painted. At the hospital they spent 30 minutes inspecting the wards before returning to the City station.

Wednesday evening's miscellaneous concert began with Mozart's "Jupiter" symphony. It received a respectful but not enthusiastic reception. The remainder of the first part was then occupied with Stanford's "Elegiac Ode". The libretto had been taken from Walt Whitman's "Burial Hymn". Some felt the text to be inappropriate for "the divine art of music". Stanford received a cordial welcome as he entered the hall and after the performance, was recalled by rapturous applause from the audience.

The second part consisted of 11 items, beginning with a concert overture in F major by Thomas Wingham who conducted the performance. This "very pleasing" work was well received. After a "Romanza" by Ponchielli and a song from Wagner's "Meistersingers", Horace came forward to conduct his "elegantly written" part song "The Calm". The chorus took this opportunity to give a hearty reception to their trainer as he made his way to the rostrum. But it was Emma Nevada who won the evening's accolade. Her singing of "Charmant Oiseau" from David's opera "La Perle de Brésil" was brilliantly executed, especially in the higher registers, leading some to proclaim her the best songstress of all time.

Thursday morning was devoted to the "Rose of Sharon"; the composer, Alexander Mackenzie, conducting. The work was a happy admixture of classic dignity and modern freedom, indicating a new path for composers to follow. Except for a few slips by the orchestra, no other fault could be found in this magnificent performance. At the close the ladies in the audience and of the chorus pelted Mackenzie with roses which had adorned their costume as thunderous applause filled the hall.

In the evening several new works were heard for the first time in the city. Benedict conducted a march "Camp Life" but the piece was considered rather common place and more suited to a military band. Mr. Maas, the tenor soloist, sang "Apollo's Invocation" composed especially for him by Massenet. Cowen conducted his "Scandinavian" symphony and Barnby his arrangement of "It was a lover and his lass".

The traditional rendering of the "Messiah" took place on Friday morning. In the evening the Prince and Princess returned to the city, arriving at the station at 8.40 pm. Escorted by the 4th Hussars, they proceeded to St. Andrew's Hall by their previous route. Mendelssohn's "Walpurgis Night" was in full flow when they entered the hall and a brief interval was taken until the Royal guests were seated. In honour of the occasion ladies had donned their most brilliant toilettes, creating a most imposing sight. After Edward Bunnett's part song "The Rhineland" there was a change to the programme. At the request of the Prince of Wales part of the "Rose of Sharon" was performed; Mackenzie being received with loud applause. A final section of more light hearted music followed, entitled "Characteristic and Humorous Music" it featured pieces such as Michaelis' "Turkish Patrol". After Berlioz stirring march from "Faust" the National Anthem brought the festival to a close and the Royal party retired to their chambers. The cheering was so loud and prolonged no demonstration of favour was shown towards the conductor, performers or solo artists.

The festival committee as a mark of their appreciation gave Alberto Randegger an extra £50 in addition to his fee of £105 (17) and £700 was donated to local charities.

Shortly after the festival the preliminary examinations for the Norfolk Scholarship were held in Norwich. 10 candidates presented themselves. At the final examination on 13th December 1884 organ student Arnold D. Culley of Great Yarmouth was awarded the first R. C. M. Norfolk Scholarship.

* This building was frequently used as an auction room.

CHAPTER 37

Explosion at Victoria Station

Horace's oratorio "Nehemiah" received 2 performances in 1885. Since premiered by the Diss Choral Society in 1879, the work had been revised and published by Joseph Williams of London. The first performance of the revised work was given by the Lynn Philharmonic Society on 30th January. The usual meeting place, the Music Hall, was otherwise occupied and so the theatre had to be converted into a suitable concert room. The orchestra pit was covered over to form a solid floor, decked with chairs and benches it helped to accommodate the large audience. A raised gallery was constructed on the stage for the chorus. "Nehemiah" had been carefully rehearsed under the leadership of its "talented" composer and the performance was most agreeable. At its conclusion loud and universal applause filled the theatre. It was evident this appreciative demonstration was most gratifying to Horace as he bowed his acknowledgement from the conductor's rostrum.

A few days later Horace conducted the Norwich Philharmonic's 68th concert in the Noverre Room. Haydn's "Surprise" Symphony, Massenet's Entr'acte "Sevillana" and Romberg's overture in D major formed part of the programme.

After another Good Friday "Messiah" Horace's attention turned to the Diss Choral Society's spring concert. Their miscellaneous programme commenced with Haydn's "Surprise" Symphony. Mr. Septimus Hewson of the cathedral choir was making his debut before a Diss audience. His enchanting performance of Sullivan's "Lost Chord" brought forth demands for an encore; the audience's persistent calls could only be silenced by Horace who commanded them to stop for he did not want to extend an already lengthy programme. Later in the evening Hewson's rendering of the "Irish Emigrant" received a similar demonstration. This time Horace relented and Hewson, to everybody's amazement whistled "Home Sweet Home". It brought further demands for an encore and Hewson obliged by whistling yet another tune of a similar style. This highly successful concert concluded with Mendelssohn's "Wedding March".

On 10th June 1885 the death of Sir Julius Benedict was announced. He had died suddenly at his home No 2 Manchester Square, London at 8 am on 5th June in the presence of his young wife and his daughter from his first marriage, Mrs. Simpson. He also left an infant son Albert Victor. In March Benedict had suffered a bronchial attack and an "infection" of the heart but his condition improved to such an extent that he was able to resume his professional duties. The funeral took place on 11th June. Despite the pouring rain a large crowd gathered in Manchester Square and also at his graveside in Kensal Green cemetery to pay their last respects.

In the autumn of 1885 the Rev. William Nottidge Ripley relinquished his duties as vicar of St. Giles, Norwich for an honorary canonry at the cathedral. His departure was marked by the presentation of an illuminated address in Earlham Hall. The volume, bound in morocco by Fletcher and Son, was tastefully decorated and bore the signatures of the curate, churchwardens, school teachers, church officers and the organist Horace Hill.

The year concluded with a second performance of "Nehemiah". A large audience assembled in St. Andrew's Hall on the evening of Thursday 10th December to hear the festival chorus perform the oratorio, with Mr. W. H. Brereton and Miss Georgina Boot taking the most arduous parts. The lady's voice possessed a great purity of tone and she soon won the affections of the audience. Although no encores were requested, those assembled seemed quite satisfied with this "scholarly" composition for Horace was recalled to acknowledge their approval.

Crowds gathered as usual in the Market Place on New Year's Eve but to their disappointment, found the instrumental bands which customarily entertained, absent. Only the bells of St. Peter Mancroft rang out the old and in with the new.

At half past three on Tuesday 26th January 1886 the occupants of Horace's St. Stephen's home could not have escaped from the sound of a terrifying explosion just a short distance away. A section of the roof of the Victoria station had suddenly blown apart. A column of smoke rose 30 feet into the air. Mr. Platford the station master was in his sitting room. The force of the blast shattered his window and knocked over furniture. The disaster happened in a room being refitted as a goods clerks' office. It had been empty for some time and was formerly the board room of the Eastern Union Railway. The explosion had destroyed the roof of the office and part of the walls. Glass canopies on the platform had also shattered and the portico entrance was damaged.

A carpenter, Mr. John Amis, had been employed to remove a section of floor boards to let in a mat. When Mr. Edward Youells, the porter entered the room he smelt gas, but Amis declared "I don't smell anything". They left and the door was locked. Youells was concerned and took Mr. Hammond, the station's goods manager into the room. Hammond detected a slight smell but decided it was nothing to worry about and suggested the carpenter should remove some more floor boards on his return. Youells was still not satisfied and went to see the foreman, Mr. Gillingwater. The room was again investigated and a window opened. The 2 gentlemen had only just left when the explosion rocked the station. John Amis was questioned. Although he recalled seeing the pipes under the floor when about his business, he denied touching them. The only injury sustained was to Mr. Platford who received a slight cut to his face from flying glass..

On 14th April yet another spectacular disaster occurred; this time on Mousehold. At the beginning of the year contractor, Mr. Denne of Walmer, Kent, had begun work on the first section of the new prison. It was to take 18 months to complete and when occupied, the other sections were to be built by prison labour. The workmen's tools were housed in a store room 20ft by 12ft. On this Wednesday evening flames engulfed the wooden building with its brick chimney and fireplace. No water was at hand and the lurid glare in the sky brought many spectators. The clerk of the works bravely retrieved the plans and documents before the store was reduced to ashes.

A week later one of the prison walls suddenly collapsed claiming the life of workman Mr. Matthew Barrett.

In North Walsham on 27th April, the amateur music society under the direction of Horace, gave a performance of Benedict's "St. Cecilia". The soloists on this occasion were Marie Phillips of London, Miss Bertha Alden of Norwich, Mr. James Gawthrop of Her Majesty's Chapel Royal and Mr. Edwin J. Bell of Westminster Abbey. Works by Vieuxtemps, Chopin and Berlioz were performed in the second part of the concert. A high state of efficiency was evident throughout.

Ponchielli's "Dance of the Hours" from his opera "Gioconda" was heard for the first time in Norwich on 4th June in the Noverre Room, performed by the Norwich Philharmonic Society. It was a rather ambitious undertaking and a little beyond their capabilities but the large attendance never the less enjoyed the experience. Haydn's "Letter Q" symphony, which followed, was however exceedingly well played. Horace's overture "May Morning" in the key of D major, a most spirited and original work, was also a success. Calls from the audience brought Horace on to the platform to bow his acknowledgements. The vocal contributions on this occasion were by the Misses Palmer and the Rev. E. J. Alvis, all being "most artistically" accompanied on the piano by James Mottram.

The festival chorus, under their skilful trainer, was being prepared for their next concert on 29th October when Beethoven's Mass in C and a selection from Handel's greatest vocal works were to be performed. On this Friday evening St Andrew's Hall was filled by a large and fashionable audience among them was Alberto Randegger. It proved to be a very successful and enjoyable evening.

The year drew to a close with the Rev. Canon Ripley chairing a discussion in the Assembly Room of the Agricultural Hall, on whether the sale of intoxicating drink on Sundays should be banned. It was thinly attended.

CHAPTER 38

Jubilee Celebrations

1887 was a year full of celebrations to mark Queen Victoria's jubilee. Norwich buzzed with joyous activity. Amid this air of jubilation Horace lost another colleague, George Brittain, who died on 24th February aged 66. George had been involved with choral singing since the days of the old Norwich Choral Society and had been part of the committee who wound up the society's affairs in 1875. He held the post of organist at Earlham parish church, St. Matthew's Thorpe Hamlet and the Octagon. Horace stood at the graveside* on the Rosary on Tuesday 1st March in the company of Edward Bunnett, James Mottram and William Heaver, to pay his last respects. He had already conducted a Philharmonic Society concert at the beginning of February where a performance of Mendelssohn's overture to "The Son and a Stranger" formed part of the programme and was in the process of preparing the North Walsham Amateur Music Society for their April miscellaneous concert.

On Wednesday the 4th May, Horace conducted another Philharmonic Society concert. The Noverre Room was well filled. This programme commenced with Haydn's 8th Salomon symphony in E♭ but some of the members of the band were not paying attention to their conductor and several obvious errors occurred. Horace tactfully drew them together and their playing improved for the second item, Kalliwoda's symphony No 4 in C. A new march by local amateur composer Richard Price was also exceedingly well played from the manuscript. Price was organist of Wangford church and a competent cellist, displaying the latter of these talents in an arrangement of Gounod's "Chanson de Magali" from the opera "Mirella" for violin, cello, piano and harmonium where he was assisted by F. W. B. Noverre, Rev. T. S. Shaw and Horace Hill.

June 21st 1887 was "Jubilee Day". In Norwich 11,000 children celebrated the occasion by singing in the Market Place. All the songs had been memorised as no leaflets were to be permitted. At 9.15am scholars over 8 years of age gathered at their schools, each bringing with them a mug. After partaking of light refreshment provided by the mayor, Harry Bullard; a "Jubilee Medal" was attached to each child by means of a ribbon and safety pin. On the front of this souvenir was a profile of the Queen surrounded by the inscription "In Commemoration of H. G. M. Queen Victoria 1837-1887" and on the reverse "Presented by Harry Bullard, Mayor of Norwich". At a pre-set time in various districts around the city, processions of children formed, 4 abreast. Each group, led by a junior teacher carrying a coloured flag: a brass band and a school banner, marched their designated route to the Market Place. South Heigham district being led by a blue flag; Lakenham, a red flag; St. George's, a green flag; North Heigham, a yellow flag; Pockthorpe, Carrow and Thorpe Hamlet, a white flag and New Catton, a red and white flag. Along the highly decorated routes, people waved and cheered as the children passed. In the Market Place Messrs. Chamberlin & Co. had covered the walls of their store with stars, shields and miniature flags. Hot house plants and palms adorned the balconies. Beneath draped a deep crimson valance edged with gold, which served as a backdrop for evergreens, flowers and a portrait of the Queen. In the centre was a large cream square bearing the words "God Bless Our Gracious Queen" in chocolate and light blue lettering. All around the Market Place bunting and banners gaily fluttered from the buildings.

Between 11.00am and 2.30pm all carriage traffic was prohibited from the area. The growing crowds of spectators were kept at bay by strong barricades, whilst the more adventurous clambered onto the roof tops.

Shortly after 11.20am the mayor and civic dignitaries, having attended a Thanksgiving Service at the cathedral, arrived at the Guildhall, entering by the north door. At the same time the first procession of 1393 children appeared and proceeded to their allotted enclosure, indicated by a flag of the same colour.

As more processions arrived the bands took up separate positions. Some outside the Albion and Waterloo hostelries with others near the Guildhall and the fish market steps.

At 12.15pm a loud cheer rose up as the civic procession left the Guildhall and proceeded along a roped pathway to a large platform erected around Wellington's monument. A joyous peal of bells rang out from St. Peter Mancroft and amid a roar of excitement the mayor took his place on the platform alongside his wife and family, the Dean of the Cathedral, Dr. Bunnett and Dr. Horace Hill. A bugle call brought perfect silence. The mayor ascended a rostrum erected 4 feet higher than the main structure and addressed the crowd, gazing down on a sea of happy young faces. Such a sight had never before been witnessed in the city.

Dr. Horace Hill then took up this elevated position to conduct the massive congregation of juvenile singers. Banners and flags were instantly lowered and furled so everyone had a clear view of the conductor's baton. On Horace's command the singing of the National Anthem filled the air. When the last strains had died away the mayor stepped forward to request 3 cheers to the Queen. 3 deafening "Hurrahs" echoed around the market place and it was several seconds before silence could be restored. Horace raised his baton for the first song, "God Bless the Prince of Wales" and hearty singing burst forth. After a further bout of cheering, "Now pray we for our country" and "Home Sweet Home" were heartily sung. Sir Harry then came forward to say "As there is no place like home, I must ask you dear children, to sing that song once again". They enthusiastically complied with his wish. At the request of the Chairman of the Norwich School Board, Mr. George White, 3 cheers for the mayor were heartily raised and this memorable occasion was brought to a close by the singing of the "Old 100th".

The children marched back by the same routes. 25 minutes passed before the last child stepped from the Market Place.

At 4 pm a special tea for the children was laid on in the school rooms, courtesy of the mayor.

In the evening the jubilee celebrations continued with a grand fireworks display on Castle Hill, its commencement being signalled by the discharge of roman candle by the mayor from a position near the castle porch. Inside the prisoners still awaited their transfer to Plumstead Rd.* The entertainment was interrupted for a short time when a fire broke out at the Jolly Farmers Inn but the blaze was quickly extinguished.

* Grave of George Brittain plot G1/1201A
* On Tuesday 2nd August 1887 the male and female prisoners incarcerated in the castle were removed by special vans to Plumstead Rd. prison. The empty castle was opened to the general public at an admission charge of 3d before work began on its conversion into a museum.
Shortly after work had commenced an ancient vaulted apartment was revealed containing stout posts, beside of which laid 2 human skulls.

CHAPTER 39

Letter from G.A. Macfarren

The local R.A.M examination certificates were presented publicly for the first time on 30th July 1887. The ceremony, conducted by the sheriff, F. Oddin Taylor, took place in the council chambers of the Guildhall at 3.00pm in the presence of Sir W. and Lady Vincent, Dr. Bunnett and the local R. A. M. representative, Dr. Horace Hill. The sheriff, in his opening speech, related how his own mother had received her musical training at the Academy from Dr. Crotch and Cipriani Potter. Horace then sketched out the progression made by the R.A.M, to those assembled. Since 1881, 149 local students had put themselves forward for examinations, 81 of whom achieved success.

After the presentation of certificates by the sheriff and a vote of thanks to Horace for his energy and commitment to the movement, a letter was read to the meeting:-

"My Dear Dr. Hill,

I am glad to learn that you are to have a public distribution at Norwich of the local certificates which I think will add to the interest of their reception. It is highly important to the value of the occasion that the Sheriff will be so kind as to deliver the awards. I beg that you will offer to that gentleman the best thanks of the committee for undertaking the duty. Much pleasure should I have in witnessing the ceremony, I am sorry to say it will be out of my power to be present and that there is none of our professors to whom the visit will be possible after our holidays have begun.

Yours with kind regards

G. A. Macfarren"

It was hoped this form of presentation would continue as an annual event with those who succeeded Taylor in office, presiding at the ceremony.

With only 3 months to the next festival, Horace attended frequent rehearsals. Of late their interim concerts had been poorly attended yielding little financial gain. The festival however offered the attraction of new works composed expressly for the occasion.

The opening concert on the frosty evening of Tuesday 11th October was honoured with the presence of the mayor, the sheriff and many corporation officials. The civic sword and mace were on display in front of the orchestra. A special telephone line linked

St. Andrew's Hall with the blind asylum giving the inmates an opportunity to listen to the musical pleasures of the festival.

After Randegger and the principal performers had assumed their positions amidst enthusiastic cheering, the programme commenced with Dr. Mackenzie's "Jubilee Ode". This boisterous work had no real musical value but was simply included to mark the occasion. The opening chorus "50 Years Our Queen" was forcefully rendered, accompanied somewhat noisily by the band. A succession of solos and choruses in a similar vein followed until the work concluded with the first verse of the National Anthem plus an additional verse to words written by the work's librettist, Joseph Bennett. At its first performance in the Crystal Palace, salvos of artillery fire had been discharged but in St. Andrew's Hall, drums acted as a substitute.

After the stormy clashes and bangs of the Ode a more tranquil mode of harmony prevailed with Saint Saëns' setting of Psalm XIX "The Heavens Declare" and Mendelssohn's "Hymn of Praise" occupying the remainder of the programme. Bottesini's devotional oratorio "The Garden of Olivet" (originally to be entitled Gethesemane) and a cantata "Isaiah" by Mancinelli were performed on Wednesday and Thursday mornings respectively. Both of these works, conducted by their composer, were warmly received. At the conclusion, each was recalled again and again before being allowed to retire.

On Thursday evening Stanford opened the concert by conducting his "Irish" symphony in F minor amid the distraction of a bustling audience who had only come to listen to Sullivan's "Golden Legend" which was to follow. Originally Stanford's choral ballad "The Revenge" had been selected but Sullivan objected, insisting only instrumental music could precede his work. When Sullivan entered to conduct his cantata, he walked with difficulty and throughout the performance sat in the conductor's chair. At its conclusion he showed signs of severe physical weakness. After the traditional performance of the "Messiah" on Friday morning to a densely crowded hall, the festival was brought to a close in the evening with Berlioz "Faust".

On the Saturday of the following week, the Norwich Philharmonic held their A. G. M. at Fasola's Café having first partaken of supper. The proprietor C. Fasola, was the founder of the Café Royal at Brighton. His premises at 59 London Street* opened for business from 9am until 11 pm serving joints between

12.30pm and 3pm, grilled steaks and chops at all times with soups, fish and entrees, until 11pm. The establishment also boasted a ladies cloakroom and gentlemen's lavatories.

Just 2 days after this social gathering, on the last day of October, Horace's dear friend G. A. Macfarren, the Principal of the R.A.M. died. The news was closely followed by that of the death of Jenny Lind Goldschmidt who passed away at her home Wynd's Point on 2nd November aged 67. Both funerals took place on Saturday 5th. November.

Jenny Lind was buried at Gt. Malvern cemetery following a choral service at the Priory church. Lowered into the grave on her coffin was a myrtle wreath from her husband Otto, made from a shrub grown from a sprig of her wedding wreath and a floral lyre from the children of the Jenny Lind Infirmary, Norwich.

The mortal remains of Macfarren were interred in West Hampstead cemetery with a commemoration service held afterwards at Westminster Abbey. A fund was set up for a scholarship in his memory, Horace being the receiver of any local contributions; himself subscribing the sum of 2 guineas.

* In May 1889 C. Fasola had a billiard room erected at the rear of his property, which could either be entered by a passageway on the western boundary or from inside the café. The room measured 34 feet by 22 feet and contained 2 billiard tables. A spacious lantern in the roof provided day light and ornamental gas jets were used at night. The walls were coloured in a light green tint with a stained and varnished dado. Plush leather upholstered furniture, adequate ventilation and sanitary "arrangements" added to the comfort of the clientele.

CHAPTER 40

Horace at the Crystal Palace

The Norwich Philharmonic Society commenced 1888 with a concert on 18th January. Haydn's symphony in G, known as the "Letter V", opened the programme. On the whole the work was well played, except for the few bars where the string section tried to race the conductor. Throughout Mozart's "Haffner" symphony, Mendelssohn's "Hebrides" overture and the overture from Herman's "La Couronne d'Or," Horace's baton was carefully watched and obeyed. The vocal services of the soprano Miss Fusselle L.R.A.M. had been secured for the evening. It was the first time this pupil of Miss Sainton Dolby had sung before a Norwich audience and her powerful singing of Cowen's "The Children's Home" won an encore. Horace's son Claud, a student at the R.A.M, accompanied at the piano.

In the November of the previous year Horace had assisted with the formation of a choral society at East Dereham. Their first public concert took place towards the end of January 1888 in the Corn Hall. The building had been metamorphosised by Mr. H. J. Warren into a comfortable concert room and Mr. Alexander had kindly put at the committee's disposal his entire stock of fabric for the drapes around the room. Under the conducting of Horace Hill, Mendelssohn's "As the Hart Pants" was successfully performed. Two works composed by the conductor were also

Crystal Palace

included in the programme, his part song "The Calm" and the quartet "He is Blessed" from his cantata "Song of Praise" of 1869. The latter being sung quite satisfactorily by Miss Nunn, Miss Acton, Mr. H.Thouless and Mr. F. A.Tipple, despite Miss Nunn being extremely nervous.

A second concert followed on Thursday 12th April when a selection from "Judas Macabaeus" featured in the programme. Richard Price had the occasion to display his mastery of the violoncello in Davidoff's "Romance and Maznita" and Claud Hill performed Schumann's Novelletto in E for piano.

The 10th Handel Festival took place at the Crystal Palace in July 1888. A special excursion was available for the sum of 16/6d from Norwich's new station at Thorpe. The price included a first class day return ticket to the Crystal Palace and entry to the festival. Those planning a longer stay in the capital could take advantage of a return ticket to Liverpool Street station for 15/- first class, 9/- second class and 7/6d for third class travel.

The final grand rehearsal on Friday 22nd July attracted 19,000 visitors. Among the chorus of 3514 of the country's finest singers were Dr. and Mrs. Horace Hill.

Before the commencement of "Messiah" in the first concert on Monday 25th, the "Dead March" from "Saul" was played in memory of the late German Emperor, followed by the National Anthem. The first verse of the anthem was sung by 780 soprani; the second verse by 771 contralti, one of whom was Mrs. Hill, and the final verse by the full chorus. 22,522 people filled the auditorium.

"Very threatening" weather was blamed for Wednesday's reduced attendance of 21,249. For this second concert a selection of pieces from lesser known works had been chosen. These, although not performed chronologically, spanned Handel's entire career from his first opera "Almira" written in 1705 to his last oratorio "Triumph of Time and Truth" of 1757. Handel's organ concerto No.7 was also admirably played with W. T. Best presiding at the Palace organ. The final concert on Friday, "Israel in Egypt", drew the largest attendance: 23,722. Throughout the festival the concerts had been expertly conducted by Mr. A. Manns who had acceded Michael Costa in 1883.

At the end of the year the R.C.M. Norfolk Scholarship was contested. To qualify for entry one had to be either a native of Norfolk or a resident of 5 years standing. 7 candidates were

August Manns

examined in Blackfriars' Hall by Dr. Hill, Dr. Bunnett and Mr. Stonex of Great Yarmouth. Three were chosen to go forward for further examination at the College. The successful candidate was Edith Gertrude Marion Tatham of St. Paul's Vicarage, East Moulsey, late of Gt. Ryburgh Rectory. Only desiring an honorary scholarship she generously handed the money to Miss Bachelder who had stood second. The College had the authority to terminate a scholarship at any time should progress or conduct prove unsatisfactory, but Norfolk's first scholar, Arnold Culley had set such a praiseworthy example, he was awarded an extra year's study.

During 1888 Horace formed a musical society in the parish of St. Stephen, Norwich. Their second public concert, in Mr. Noverre's Assembly Room took place on Friday 18th January 1889 supported by a large audience of friends and neighbours. The cantatas "May Day" by Macfarren and Fox's "The Jackdaw of Rheims" were most enjoyably performed. All the proceeds from the concert went towards the funding of a nurse to attend the poor of the parish.

The previous evening Horace had been at East Dereham conducting a choral society concert. Cowen's "The Rose Maiden" formed the first part. Claud Hill accompanied the ballads and songs of the miscellaneous second part which included "Goodwin Sands" by S. Adams sung by baritone Mr. Charles King who, although suffering from hoarseness, faithfully fulfilled his obligation.

Towards the end of May the Edison phonograph was demonstrated in the Assembly Room of the Agricultural Hall. A previous attempt to show the powers of the instrument in St. Andrew's Hall had failed, consequently the attendance on this Friday evening was only "fair". Lecturer, Mr. William Lynd opened the proceedings by stating the instrument he had brought along no longer qualified as the "latest perfected phonograph", for a more sophisticated and sensitive instrument had been produced which could detect the sounds of breathing and heart beat. This new model, however, was not yet available for exhibition. He explained how in the future Edison hoped to perfect a pocket sized phonograph, people could then record the voices of the principal artists in the concert room and take them away. The audience found his suggestion so ludicrous that laugher revolved round the room. A practical illustration was then given and their laughter turned to amazement as the sound of a cornet solo, post horn calls and a German street band burst from the phonograph. Lynd spoke of how the equipment would be of use to lawyers, clergymen, doctors and journalists. Already a talking newspaper had been perceived. It could also prove to be an excellent aid in teaching foreign languages. To demonstrate further Trumpeter Addis, of the 20th Hussars, positioned himself in front of a large funnel and proceeded to play J. S. Lee's cornet solo "Souvenir de Balincollig". The phonograph then reproduced the exact sound. This was the very first recording made outside London. It was feared the general public viewed Edison's work with suspicion so special permission had been granted to record at the Norwich lecture. The atmosphere within the hall had turned from disbelief to excitement. Mr. George White and Mr. Chamberlin united with Mr. Lynd before the funnel. Clapping their hands they shouted "Bravo, Bravo, Bravo". Every sound was captured.

Interest in the temperance movement though outweighed that of the phonograph. In October crowds gathered in the city for the anniversary meeting of the Diocesan Branch of Church of England Temperance Society.

A service was held in the cathedral at 11 o'clock. At 1 o'clock some 300 people partook of luncheon in Blackfriars' Hall followed by a conference in St. Andrew's Hall. Crowds flooded into the city for the evening meeting. St. Andrew's Hall became packed and Blackfriars' Hall was opened for the overflow. It too was quickly filled and 100's of people were turned away. Horace had formed a volunteer choir of 400 voices to sing hymns during the evening. He conducted the choir before this multitude of people who had come to hear the Lord Bishop of Norwich, the Lord Bishop of London and a medical doctor, Mr. Carpenter, speak on the dangers of alcohol.

In 1889 Horace's position as local examiner for the R.A.M. ceased when the Academy joined with the R.C.M. to form the Associated Board. At his last examination session on 6th and 7th May, Horace and Mr. Arthur O'Leary of the Academy examined 54 candidates. In November 1889 Mr. F. Oddin Taylor of The Close became the Associated Board's honorary representative for the district.

CHAPTER 41

Rabies.

The Collegiate School for Girls' on Newmarket Rd held their annual prize giving in January 1890. The proceedings commenced with a vocal and instrumental concert in which the pupils participated, one of whom was Miss M. Hill. Dr. Horace Hill conducted.

An influenza epidemic had begun to hit the city but despite this the Norwich Philharmonic managed to go ahead with their 78th concert on 12th February. Horace was suffering from the effects of the illness but was still quite energetic at the conductor's desk as he directed symphonies by Haydn and Kalliwoda, the overture from Schubert's opera "Alphonso and Estrella" and a March by Lachner.

On the day before the Philharmonic's 79th concert of 22nd May 1890, where Romberg's bright and cheerful symphony in E♭ was performed, Sims Reeves gave his farewell concert in St. Andrew's Hall. The concert had originally been planned for Easter week of 1883 but Reeves caught a chill and consequently the event did not take place. This time however the numerous audience found him in fine voice as he sang "The Jolly Young Waterman", "Come into the Garden Maud", Lindsey Lennox's "Dream Memories" and Dibdin's "Tom Bowling". All 4 songs were encored. An identical concert had taken place 2 days previous at the Aquarium in Great Yarmouth, both were promoted by Mr. Nightingale, lessee of the Aquarium.

Having survived influenza Norwich citizens faced the fear of rabies as several cases of the disease were diagnosed near New Buckenham. Both children and adults had been bitten by a liver and white spaniel. The city and county councils, on 30th June, ordered all dogs to be muzzled. The offending animal was eventually shot near New Buckenham. 8 victims were sent to the Pasteur Institute in Paris for treatment, their expenses being paid from a subscription fund which collected £103. All survived. The muzzling order remained in place until after the musical festival. (13)

Since the festival of 1887 changes had been made. There had been a reintroduction of the "nursery" classes under F. C. Brookes F.C.O. for the training of singers to chorus standard and also a return to 3 festival chorus concerts each year, which of late had become rather infrequent.

To ensure the success of the 1890 festival Horace insisted all members of the chorus attended rehearsals regularly and were prepared to work exceptionally hard throughout the month of September, thus enabling a short break to renew their strength and energy for the arduous week ahead.

At about this time Horace relinquished his position as organist at St. Giles'. In 1887 his salary had increased to £30 per annum. He was superseded by S Bennett (12).

As the festival approached the main city streets hung with bunting. Mayor Dakin's business premises in Davey Place was tastefully adorned with flags, the city coat of arms and the words "Success to our Festival" worked in dull gold lettering upon a crimson ground. Between the 1st floor windows the names and year of birth of the composers featuring in the festival were similarly displayed. To the left appeared the names of Handel, Bach, Spohr, Auber, Weber and Rossini. To the right, Mendelssohn, Wagner, Sullivan, Mackenzie, Parry and MacCunn.

The premises of Alderman Wild in the Haymarket were also notably decorated. A centre shield carried the names of Hill, Bunnett, Mackenzie, Parry and Sullivan. A quotation from Milton's "Allegro" was flanked by the dates 1824 and 1890. Wednesday proved to be the most interesting day of the festival. Visitors made their way to the hall in pouring rain which roared down as they listened to the symphony from the second part of Spohr's "The Last Judgement". The work was followed by a "perfect treat", "Lamentatio Daviddi" by Schutz. The bass soloist Franco Novara took up a position close to the organ. Surrounded by 4 trombonists, Messrs. C. Hadfield, C. Geard, W. T. Blamphin, and Albert Phasey; accompanied by Dr. Bunnett at the organ, he sang the Latin text. The solemnity and dignity of the music contrasted so greatly with that which had gone before, it was found inexpressibly touching.

The piece was followed by Parry's new work "L'Allegro ed il Pensieroso", which had been written especially for the festival; the composer receiving rapturous applause as he took his place on the orchestra. After a short repose for luncheon when the sky brightened, Rossini's "Stabat Mater" brought the programme to a close.

The Wednesday evening concert was devoted entirely to 2 works by A. C. Mackenzie, both conducted by the composer. His incidental music to "Ravenswood", written for the dramatised adaptation of Walter Scott's novel "The Bride of Lammermoor" was performed for the first time in a concert room. The second part of the programme featured his cantata "Dream of Jubal" with actress Julia Neilson as the narrator.

Friday morning brought a break with tradition, "Elijah" being performed instead of the "Messiah" but the morning still drew the largest attendance of the week.

After the festival, Horace and the chorus still had work to do for they had consented to given 2 further concerts for the poor of the city. When asked by the mayor if they would give their services, they unanimously agreed. Local soloists Miss Agnes Larkcom, Mrs. Legge, Miss Meredyth Elliott, Hirwen Jones and Mr. R. Hilton joined forces with the cathedral choir and a band of 50 local and metropolitan players, all of whom volunteered their assistance. The first of these "People's Concerts" was held on Wednesday 22nd October in St. Andrew's Hall. An audience of 1,600 paid 6d to sit closely packed together on wooden benches. The programme commenced with the singing of Costa's· arrangement of the National Anthem, followed by a selection from "Judas Maccabaeus" with additional accompaniment by Costa, the music having been loaned especially for the occasion by Messrs. Novello. Hirwen Jones was suffering with a cold and as a result his performance suffered too. By Friday morning Mr. Hilton had caught the cold. His symptoms being such that he was unable to sing. A telegram was instantly dispatched to Mr. Price of the Westminster choir who kindly accepted the engagement. Some 1650 people attended the second concert. A selection from Mendelssohn's "Hear My Prayer" and "Elijah" formed the first part of the programme.

During the interval the chorus retired to Blackfriars' Hall, where Horace read to them the following letter:-

"My Dear Dr. Hill,

The kindness to which I was treated in Norwich last week by you and my friends of the festival chorus demands a much stronger and longer letter of thanks than I can write at the present moment. But I cannot postpone the expression of my gratitude to you and your faithful, willing and enthusiastic forces for the manner in which you all interested yourselves in and helped the career of "Jubal". I am fully aware that a friendly feeling exists between us on account of former work done together. Still I was hardly prepared to find my wishes fulfilled so completely. To you, Dr.

Bunnett and your vocal friends, I am most deeply indebted not only for the excellent performance of my work but for the cordial way in which my wishes to a hint were observed faithfully. Now let me tell you that you have full reason to be satisfied with the result of your labours in connection with the festival of 1890. The great encouragement justly given, which your choir has received, will lead to great good in your county and while we recognise the strength of your hand in the work done, let us not forget each individual who assisted your high aim and helped to carry out your intentions successfully. Speaking personally, it was a real pleasure to feel that each member was willing to do his best and I freely and frankly acknowledge that I never had greater pleasure in conducting a performance than I had on the evening of 15th October. Believe me my dear Dr. Hill. Very faithfully yours A. C. Mackenzie".

Filled with this gracious compliment the chorus returned to the hall to perform various miscellaneous items. A "pretty" duet "When the Soft Spring Winds" by Horace Hill was sung by Miss Larkcom and Hirwen Jones, whose cold had notably improved. It gave much pleasure; the artists and composer being recalled amid loud applause. Before the delightful evening ended Mayor Dakin ascended the orchestra to express his gratitude to all concerned. Cheering filled the hall as each was thanked in turn for their contribution. He had always been proud of Norwich but never more so than on this occasion.

CHAPTER 42

The Norwich Philharmonic Society's 80th Concert

The Norwich Philharmonic celebrated its jubilee on Thursday 5th March 1891, their first public concert having been given on 5th March 1841. The society was founded in 1839. Prior to this a group of amateur musicians known as "The Hall Concert" flourished from 1789 until its dissolution in 1834. Several scores found their way into the Norwich Philharmonic's library, labelled as "Hall Society".

To celebrate their Jubilee the society gave its 80th concert. The Noverre Room was packed with supporters each being presented with a brochure on the history of the society to mark the occasion.

The programme commenced with Mozart's "Jupiter" symphony. Miss Ada Loaring, who was making her debut in Norwich, sang T. Cooke's "Over Hill Over Dale" and Mr. Sawford Dye Sullivan's "The Sailor's Grave". Schubert's "Unfinished" symphony and works by Handel, Weber and Beethoven filled the programme before an overture by Romberg brought the concert to a close. Horace conducted the band who had thrown their hearts and souls into the music.

At the previous evening's rehearsal a presentation had been made by Mr. Sutton on behalf of the society to Horace and Mr. F. W. B. Noverre, in recognition of the valuable time and attention each had given to the cause. Horace received a handsomely bound 5 volumed set of Grove's Dictionary of Music. The first volume bearing a label which stated, in gold lettering "Presented to Horace Hill Mus. D. by the members on the 50th anniversary of the first concert given by the Norwich Philharmonic Society in recognition of his valuable services as conductor for the past 10 years. March 5th 1891". Horace had been a member of the society since 1854.

Mr. Noverre received a framed proof of an etching by Lowenstan of a picture entitled "The Quartett" which depicted Joachim, Ries, Strauss and Piatti engaged in tuning up for a rehearsal. A tablet attached to the frame was inscribed with a suitable sentiment.

The same Wednesday evening Mr. Howlett had engaged Mde. Trebelli to sing in a concert in St. Andrew's Hall. It was thinly attended.

In May the Philharmonic Society and the festival chorus under Horace's direction assisted Dr. Bunnett with the closing concert in his popular series of organ recitals in St. Andrew's Hall. After a programme which included Guilmant's fugue in D major and Handel's organ concerto No 9 in B♭, the mayor, Mr. Wild, addressed the audience informing them that the organ needed repairs to the cost of £300 before the next series could commence. The same month the Philharmonic gave their 81st concert. This time the band was arranged differently to previous occasions, in an attempt to create a better balance of sound. The programme opened with the 1st of Haydn's Salomon symphonies, followed by 2 movements of Mendelssohn's "Reformation" symphony and the overture from Rossini's "La Cenerentola". Miss Margaret Butcher made her first appearance with the society singing Cowen's "Left Untold" and Gounod's "The Worker".

In June Horace and his wife travelled to London with 10 other local singers to again take part in the Handel Festival. Many thousands of visitors and performers found an opportunity to see the Crystal Palace's extraordinary collection of lions, tigers, panthers, cheetahs and bears performing tricks in one extremely large cage.

On his return to Norwich, Horace commenced rehearsals for the first interim concert of the festival chorus. A performance of Sullivan's oratorio "Light of the World" was given on 22nd October. This early work of Sullivan's, written in 1873, was not attractive to the public and many prominent citizens were conspicuous by their absence. The chorus had worked hard to overcome the awkward intervals and Horace had the added difficulty of conducting from a marked vocal score as the terms quoted by the proprietor for a full score were prohibitory.

The repairs and alterations to the St. Andrew's Hall organ were completed by the 7th November. Although Bryceson Bros. had been approached for an estimate, the work was carried out by the local firm of Norman Bros. and Beard. The instrument had been thoroughly cleaned, a larger capacity reservoir installed under the great organ and improvements made to the noisy tracker action. At the first of Bunnett's new series of popular recitals an audience of 1,250 heard the new Vox Humana stop. It still required attention; the upper notes being out of tune with several inclined to whistle.

As the year rolled into 1892, 2 deaths from influenza occurred in the city and citizens soon found themselves gripped by another epidemic. The severity of the outbreak disrupted the daily running of industry, railways, police and military. By the end of January the mortality rate was calculated at 44 per 1000 cases. During one night at the Great Hospital in Bishopgate, 3 victims died within an hour and a further 2 deaths occurred the following morning.

Having survived this ordeal the Norwich Philharmonic held their 82nd concert on 16th February. Amongst a programme of works by Mozart, Spohr, Grieg, Gounod, Sullivan, Nicolai and Smart was a delightful sonnet for oboe and orchestra composed at short notice, especially for the occasion by Horace Hill. The piece opened with a graceful melody for oboe in a minor key, accompanied by strings "con sordini", answered by a counter melody in the relative major for violoncello. The oboist, Mr. E. V. Davies of London was the only professional engaged; the 'cellist being Mr. R. Price. So great was the applause at its conclusion that a repeat was given with increased success. Horace's busy conducting schedule continued in March with the second of the festival chorus's interim concerts. Gounod's "The Redemption" was performed. The choice was wise as it drew an abnormally large attendance. After conducting the traditional Good Friday "Messiah" and directing the festival chorus with the Philharmonic at Bunnett's final popular recital of the series in April, Horace conducted the 83rd Philharmonic concert on 12th May. The highlight of the evening was Reinecke's Op. 188 Trio for oboe, horn and piano which was beautifully rendered by Mr. E. V. Davies, A. Borsdorf, and Kingston Rudd. Especially for the concert, Horace had composed "Benedictus", a vocal quartet with orchestral accompaniment. Its performance was a failure, the accompaniment being far too loud causing the vocal parts to be totally inaudible.

Other compositions by Horace dating from this period met with better success for in June the London Music Publishing Co. announced the publication of "Infinite Anglican Chants" which included contributions from Horace Hill, Claud Hill, Edward Bunnett and Frank Bates, the new cathedral organist.

CHAPTER 43

The Mayor's Conversazione

On Monday 3rd October 1892 Dr. Horace Hill, Mrs. Hill and the Misses Hills were among the 1000 guests invited to the mayor's Conversazione in St. Andrew's Hall. Shortly after 8 o'clock the company began to arrive by way of the south porch entrance which had been adorned with flowers and hot house plants: oriental rugs covered the floor. A cloakroom was provided at the west end by screening off a portion of the hall. A heavily curtained doorway gave access to a reception area. The guests were greeted by the mayor Mr. G. M. Chamberlin and Mrs. Alexander Chamberlin, representing the mayoress, who was absent through the recent death of her mother. Having emerged from this dimly lit area guests were confronted by a blaze of electric light illuminating the decorations, their brightly coloured dresses and military uniforms adding to the splendid sight.

A dado of cream drapery surrounded the walls, panelled with old gold and topped with a grass green frieze, exquisitely worked with tendrils of ivy. The bases of the nave columns were similarly decorated with the addition of small gold stars and gilt geometric designs to the panels. An abundance of flags hung from the capitals. Silk banners bearing mottoes of a musical or dancing theme drooped from the arcading. At the west end a semi circular screen of large mirrors in plush frames, reflected the scene.

On the orchestra, a rich collection of "exotics" and the civic regalia were on display, backed by a semi circular screen of cream cloth with a festoon of maroon drapery looped up by sea green bands. At the rear, a grand trophy of flags rose from a shield carrying the city's armorial bearings.

The nave floor, covered in cream cloth was graced with drawing room furniture. On the floors of the north and south aisles laid crimson cloth. A dais extended the entire length of each aisle, furnished with ottomans and lounges upholstered in rich Utrecht velvet. The area between the dais and the arcading acted as a promenade.

Two rooms off the north side had been luxuriously converted into a retiring room for the ladies, and a smoking room for the gentlemen.

The walls of the corridor leading from the hall to Blackfriars' Hall were draped in cream and blue silk muslin, relieved with a maroon frieze. Rout seats gave a pleasant refuge for those wishing to retire from the main apartment.

Blackfriars' Hall had been turned into a spacious refreshment room. The walls hung with a dado of crushed strawberry silk, panelled in cream cloth, topped by a sage green festoon caught up by bands of magenta and gold. Hot house plants arranged in ornate groups filled every "nook and cranny". A buffet provided by Mr. Snelling of Rampant Horse St., stretched along the north side. In the centre of the hall, on a carpet of crimson cloth, small tables were placed for the guests' convenience. The whole scene was extended by a screen of mirrors at the east end. During the evening light music was performed under the direction of Kingston Rudd and Dr. Bunnett. After the National Anthem, the Gate House choir performed part songs, including "O Mistress Mine" by MacCunn, interspersed with organ solos. At 11 o' clock the joyful company dispersed.

The following week Adelina Patti made her first appearance before a Norwich audience, having been engaged by Messrs. Howlett for a concert in the Agricultural Hall. It was filled by 2,300 people, a further 600 occupied the galleries. Several inmates from the blind institution were in the audience having received a special invitation. As Patti made her entrance, bowing to the audience, the hall echoed with rapturous applause. After "Batti, Batti" from Don Giovanni and "Il Bacio" by Arditi the audience were surprised to hear the introduction to "Home Sweet Home". This departure from the programme was greeted with much excitement, it being sometime before Patti could commence this much loved ballad.

1892 concluded with the 3rd interim concert of the festival chorus. On 22nd November Horace conducted a performance of "Acis and Galatia" which was followed by the first performance of his new overture "Yewbarrow". The overture had been written whilst Horace was visiting his son at Grange Over Sands. A yew covered mound near to the town, offering excellent views of Morecambe Bay, provided his inspiration.

The first performance was received with much enthusiasm, Horace being twice recalled to the platform. "Yewbarrow" was considered the best of his compositions; worthy of a place in the forthcoming festival.

Adelina Patti

CHAPTER 44

Paderewski at the 1893 Festival

Horace's pupil, Amy Vincent of Great Yarmouth made several appearances in concerts conducted by her tutor during 1893. In January she sang the principal soprano part in the North Walsham Amateur Musical Society's performance of "St. Paul"; her beautiful, rich voice charming the audience. Horace was justly proud of his talented pupil.

In April, Amy and the Rev. A. E. Black of Buxton, added vocal contributions to the Norwich Philharmonic's 84th concert. Although suffering from the effects of a cold she sang "At the Minster Gates", a new piece entitled "Hope" by Claud Hill, and the rather "lackadaisical" song "I Dream't that I Dwelt in Marble Halls".

Two weeks later the young lady entertained at Dr. Bunnett's final popular recital of the season, the festival chorus and the Norwich Philharmonic also giving their assistance. Again she sang "At the Minster Gates", this time her tutor had written an accompaniment for organ and orchestra especially for the occasion.

An invitation was sent to Horace to attend a presentation to Mr. Stonex, the organist of St Nicholas, Great Yarmouth on 1st May. The gentleman was to receive £100 for his valuable services to local music. Having a prior engagement Horace wrote the following letter of apology.

"I regret that an important engagement on the 1st of May will prevent me from being present at the interesting ceremony you refer to. I entertain a high regard for Mr. Stonex not only because he has shewn such ability as an organist and as conductor of the Great Yarmouth Musical Society but also on account of his kindly disposition, which has won for him the regard of all who have had the privilege of making his acquaintance. I hope he may long be spared to enjoy the esteem of the good people of Yarmouth and to continue his labours amongst them hitherto".

Just a few yards from Horace's home at St. Stephen's Gate was the organ works of Norman Bros. and Beard. At 3 o'clock on the afternoon of Saturday 29th July 1893 the public were invited to attend a free recital in the factory given by William Stephenson Hoyte, organist of All Saints church, Margaret Street, London. Hoyte had first visited Norwich in November 1891 when he played the organ in St. Andrew's Hall to entertained the visitors to the Chrysanthemum Show. The purpose of his latest visit was to test an instrument built by the firm before its shipment to Perth in Western Australia. Music by Bach, Schumann, Guilmant and Dubois featured in the programme as well as Hoyte's own composition "Fantaisie in C minor".

Horace and the festival chorus had many new works to learn before the 1893 musical festival. The oratorio "Judith" was to be given its first performance in Norwich with Parry coming to conduct. Cowen had composed a romantic legend "The Water Lily" for soli chorus and orchestra and J. F Barnett a cantata for female voices, "The Wishing Bell"; both pieces being written especially for the festival. The band also had to grapple with new works. Edward German had composed his symphony No 2 in A minor expressly for the occasion and he too was coming to conduct. Mackenzie's "Pibroch" suite for orchestra and solo violin was also to be heard for the first time; Senor Pablo de Sarasate taking the solo part. This attractive suite used as its principal theme the Scottish air "Three Guid Fellows". At its performance Sarasate, a man in his 50's, of medium height and an abundance of grey hair, took up his position to the left of Randegger, the conductor, to play the solo part from memory. The exuberant welcome he received however affected his concentration. Only a few bars into the performance both soloist and orchestra came to a halt. The violinist referred to the score then made a successful fresh start. He was not the only person to succumb to hearty Norfolk acclamations for Luigi Mancinelli, after conducting his overture "Cleopatra", interpreted the audience's jubilant reaction as a signal for a repeat and the whole work was performed again. On the Wednesday evening the hall was filled to capacity. The oppressive heat and smell from the gas lights had gone and the hall was bathed in the far more comfortable light from electricity. The old turkey red panelling had been painted a pale blue giving the hall a brighter appearance. For the first time the ladies of the chorus, which included Mrs. Horace Hill were uniformly dressed. Contingents from Great Yarmouth and Lowestoft choral societies swelled the numbers, the former being trained under the instruction of Henry Stonex and the latter under Mr. H. D. Flowers.

The programme commenced with the overture to Wagner's "Meistersingers". The orchestra played badly; the beauty of the piece being totally lost. It was followed by Marian Mackenzie

Paderewski

singing a song from Saint Saëns' "Samson and Delilia"; her cold hampering her usual style. Then came the moment every one had been waiting for; accompanied by hearty cheering, the Polish pianist Paderewski appeared on the platform. His photograph had been displayed in many city windows and had attracted the attention of female glances. This famous virtuous took up his position on a low chair in front of an Erard concert grand piano to give the first performance in England of his "Polish Fantaisie" for piano and orchestra; his agile fingers rippling over the keys with amazing dexterity. The work, based on Polish airs, had been composed in a chalet at Yport in the space of just 3 weeks. Paderewski composing each day from 10 in the morning till 11 at night. Having completed the 150 pages of manuscript he was

195

anxious to hear his creation. Gathering together an orchestra from the locality they tried out the work in an empty building near to the chalet. The Polish violinist Gorski, volunteered to conduct. All were ready to commence when Paderewski realised there was no baton. Rushing into the chalet he emerged with a billiard cue, unscrewed the two sections and handed the smaller one to Gorski. It made an excellent substitute.

In St. Andrew's Hall Randegger chose to revert to the conventional baton. At the conclusion of a brilliant performance tremendous applause echoed around the hall; Paderewski bowing thrice in acknowledgement as the demonstration of approval continued.

With the excitement still simmering Alfred Gaul made his way on to the orchestra and bowed to his native citizens. He had written a cantata "Una" expressly for the festival but his greeting was rather subdued. It was not considered the right time or place to hear a work from a sober English composer. The performance went on longer than anticipated causing the scheduled interval to be abandoned. Horace immediately took up the baton to conduct his 8th overture "Yewbarrow". Since its first hearing much of the work had been rewritten with parts for harp and double bassoon being added. The work was well received.

At 10.30pm Paderewski returned to the platform to play Chopin's Nocturne No 12 in G and Study in F, followed by a Liszt rhapsody. Although now gone 11 o'clock he succumbed to the demand for an encore, playing "Nachtstücke in F" by Schumann. The evening concluded with the overture to "The Merry Wives of Windsor" but the performance was spoilt as many made their departure from the hall.

A month after the festival, members of the chorus were invited to a ball in their honour. St. Andrew's Hall was tastefully decorated, the appearance enhanced by magnificent displays of chrysanthemums and palms. Mr. C. J. Campling's band was in attendance, playing lancers, valses, quadrilles and polkas until the early hours.

CHAPTER 45

The Norfolk and Norwich School of Music

The residents of St. Stephen's Road were habitually plagued by the abominable nuisance of carts of all descriptions being left on the roadside between the Trowel and Hammer inn and the hospital. Whilst the horses were taken into the inn yard, the carts were not, turning this "good" road into a livery stable yard. Often the carts were two abreast forcing tradesmen delivering barrels, packages and furniture to draw up alongside them. One angry resident appealed to the council, through the newspaper, to act on this problem. He paid high rates for his property and was not prepared to live in a road which resembled an auction scene. The Hill's family home was situated next to the Trowel and Hammer. (19) Leaving the chaos behind him Horace made his usual trips to North Walsham on Tuesdays to prepare the choral society for their first concert of the year. In February 1894 a performance of his "Nehemiah" was given in the church rooms. This "capital building" for concerts was filled to capacity by an appreciative audience. The soloists on this occasion were Amy Vincent, Miss Frances Acton, Mr. H. J. Brookes from Norwich cathedral, Mr. W. D. Tomkins, Mr. J.J. Manning and the Rev. H. Wimble. Many members of the Norwich Philharmonic strengthened the band.

After successfully completing another Good Friday "Messiah", assisting Dr. Bunnett with the last of his series of popular recitals and directing the first interim concert by the festival chorus; Horace conducted the Norwich Philharmonic's 87th concert in early May. The programme included a song by Claud Hill "In Fairyland", sung by Miss May Shipley and two movements from Mendelssohn's string quartet in D major Op.44 No1, admirably played by F. W. B. Noverre, Rev. T. S. Shaw, H. Thouless and R. Price. Noverre's eldest daughter Mary was also a violinist and had recently been awarded the Norfolk and Norwich scholarship at the Royal College of Music, her father and Horace having been her previous tutors. They had yet to learn that her outstanding ability would result in her tenure being twice renewed.

Professional musicians in Norwich were becoming concerned over unqualified persons setting themselves up as music teachers. This "objectionable" practice was causing the standard of music in the city to fall. The mayor was approached and a meeting convened in the Guildhall for 17th July 1894. Here the possibilities of establishing a School of Music were discussed. Horace Hill, Edward Bunnett and Kingston Rudd were among those present. Their aim was to reverse this downward trend by awarding certificates of competency to students capable of teaching. The meeting agreed to set up a limited liability company with a capital of £1000.

At the time Horace's family were preparing for the wedding of their second son Alfred Arthur. Alfred had gained the medical qualifications of L.R.C.S. and L.R.C.P. and was living in Tunstall Staffordshire.

On 30th August 1894 Alfred Arthur married Lucie Drabble, the eldest daughter of Mr. F. C. Drabble at St. Stephen's church, Eastwood, Rotherham before a large congregation. His bride wore a dress of ivory bengaline silk trimmed with Spanish lace and orange blossom. She also carried a wreath of orange blossom and wore a conventional veil. Alfred's sister Miss M. Hill was one of the 4 bridesmaids, the other 3 being relatives of the bride. All were in dresses of light fawn with cream silk trimmings and matching picture hats. Each received a gold brooch and a beautiful bouquet from the bride groom. Brother Claud acted as groomsman. After an "at home" at the Drabble residence in Clifton Lane the newly weds left for Colwyn Bay.

Before the year of 1894 had ended, the citizens of Norwich witnessed the unveiling of a terra cotta medallion portrait of Jenny Lind at the Pottergate Infirmary by Lady Eade; the opening of the Castle Museum by the Duke and Duchess of York and heard a performance of Julius Benedict's "St. Cecilia" as part of the festival chorus's second interim concert.

Soon the city was struggling against another bitter winter as treacherous conditions hampered both vehicular and pedestrian mobility. Before venturing out, people were recommended to warm the soles of their boots in front of a fire and then apply a coating of grease to prevent the "balling" of snow underfoot. Property owners and occupiers were ordered by the Sanitary Authority to keep the pavement outside their premises clear of ice and snow. Failure to comply resulted in a £5 fine.

During these appalling conditions Paderewski made a return to the city to give a recital in St. Andrew's Hall on 31st January, under the promotion of Messrs. Howlett. Those arriving late constantly interrupted the first item, Beethoven's op.111 sonata, but once settled the large audience sat spellbound for 2 whole hours as the virtuoso performer played pieces by Chopin, Schumann, Liszt and his own "Cracovienne" from his Op. 14 composition. Many then journeyed home by the special late night trains to Yarmouth, Lowestoft, Cromer, Foulsham and Brandon calling at all intermediate stations.

The previous evening Horace braved the freezing temperatures and icy conditions to travel to North Walsham where he conducted the music society's performance of "Judith". Master F. W. Hill was one of the principal soloists.

Over the winter months Horace had been busy orchestrating the overture to his operetta "Sleeping Beauty" in readiness for the Norwich Philharmonic's 88th concert. The operetta had been performed with only a piano accompaniment in April 1894, by the pupils of the Church Company's High School in Yarmouth. On the evening of 21st February 1895 the Philharmonic band played the overture with much feeling, the graceful and pleasing themes astounding the audience. It proved so successful that another section of the work was planned for their 89th concert in May. Between these two concerts Horace's wife was engaged as the society's official accompanist. She fulfilled her role with much satisfaction to all concerned.

On 4th March 1895, just 8 months after the initial meeting, the Norfolk and Norwich School of Music was officially opened at 14 Rampant Horse St. by the mayor, Col. Bignold, in the presence of the shareholders and professors of the establishment. The Rev. Barrett of Prince's St. Congregational church, Dr. Bates, Kingston Rudd, James Mottram, W. R. C. Howlett, F. W. B. Noverre and Dr. Horace Hill were among those present. However the inclement weather had forced many to send letters of apology. After the formalities, a programme of music was given in the school's commodious concert room. Beginning with the national anthem the entertainment went on to include a "Nocturne in D flat" and a "Mazurka" from the pen of Dr. Bunnett, both played by the composer. During the interval coffee and light refreshment were available from a buffet prepared by Mr. Snelling.

An organ should have been installed for the opening but owing to the unfavourable weather the builders advised to delay this until the spring. The instrument would however be ready for lessons in the summer term. The school fees ranged from 25/- to 3 guineas per term. Each pupil receiving 40 minutes tuition per week. Evening classes were being planned for choral, orchestral, and

Rev. Barrett

harmony tuition at 12/6d per term. On a Friday evening in mid July the students gave their first concert before an audience of invited guests in the concert room attached to the side of the school. Considering the short space of time since their studies had begun the performances were highly commendable; a testimony to the careful training received. Songs were rendered by Miss Nellie Howling, Miss Florence Howling, Miss Black, Miss Hawes and Miss de Caux. Solo piano pieces were contributed by Miss Boddington, Miss Kenny and Miss Ethel White. The latter, with Miss Mable Harrington, also played the duet "Hommage á Handel" Op. 92 by Moscheles. The evening concluded with professors Kingston Rudd and Arthur Bent performing 2 movements from Beethoven's "Kreutzer" sonata.

Horace was now the local representative for the London College of Music. In the autumn of 1895 the College used the School of Music as an examination centre. The examiner was G. A. Holmes.

CHAPTER 46

Dr. Bunnett's Jubilee

A new style of tuition was introduced at the commencement of the Norfolk and Norwich School of Music's spring term on 20th January 1896. The original lessons of 40 minutes individual tuition still continued but students also had the option to be taught in groups of 3, each receiving 20 minutes personal instruction plus a further 40 minutes listening to the instruction imparted to the other 2 group members. This method enabled fees to be reduced, making musical tuition within reach of a wider section of the community.

At the suggestion of the school's secretary William Heaver, the students volunteered to entertain the patients in the Norfolk and Norwich hospital and on the evening of Tuesday 25th February 1896 a concert was given in a vacant ward for those sufficiently convalesced to be moved.

Out of the 18 items performed 11 were by the students. Horace Hill and Kingston Rudd accompanied songs sung by Miss de Caux, Miss Hawes and Miss Howling on a piano lent for the occasion by Messrs. Howlett and Sons. Mr. R. Burrows and the orchestra class performed a "Sonnet" for oboe and strings composed by Horace Hill. The work had previously been played by the students at their last end of term concert. Mr. Bosworth Harcourt added variety to the programme by reciting "The Bishop and the Caterpillar" and "The Enchanted Shirt". At the close of the concert the Rev. Duckett, on behalf of the board of management and the patients, thanked all those who had taken part.

The school's concert room hosted a meeting of the eastern section of the Incorporated Society of Musicians on the afternoon of Wednesday 8th April 1896 when a paper was read by Henry Charles Banister, professor of the R.A.M. entitled "Some thoughts concerning musical composition". Dr. Bunnett chaired the meeting, announcing that owing to the unavoidable absence of Dr. Mann the musical illustrations would be provided by Richard Lowne, (a former pupil of Bunnett's).

The school's spring term closed on 16th April 1896 with another concert. On this occasion Horace's daughter Mildred played the piano, giving a performance of the "Barcarole" from Sterndale Bennett's 4th concerto. A "Cavatina" for flute and orchestra, composed by Horace's son Claud was also featured in the programme. This cleverly written piece first appeared in the Norwich Philharmonic's 90th concert in February 1896.

Before the commencement of the summer term on 4th May, Horace witnessed a presentation to his dear friend Dr. Bunnett, in honour of his 50 years devoted service to music, having made his public debut on 16th September 1845 in the Norfolk and Norwich Festival. Bunnett had advertised his achievement in September 1895 when, to mark his jubilee, he presented his friends with a card containing the following words :-

"To My Lyre
(on attaining its jubilee)
Kindly has time thro 50 changeful years,
Left in my hands the lyre so dear to me,
Fresh to my view each string to-day appears,
Fresh as when first it breathed out melody
Speak, then, my lyre! and tell to each who hears
Meet is thy voice to sing thy jubilee!"

The words he had set to music; the whole forming a personal momento of the occasion. In the December of 1895 the mayor and corporation had met in the Guildhall to establish a subscription list for Bunnett's testimonial. Saturday 18th April 1896 was chosen for the presentation, it being his last popular recital of the season. That evening St. Andrew's Hall was filled to capacity. On the orchestra, members of the Norwich Philharmonic and the festival chorus assembled with their conductor, Horace Hill. As the National Anthem was played, the mayor, deputy mayor and members of the corporation entered in procession to take up their positions. A programme of music to suit all tastes had been arranged. The organ solos included the overture from "Samson" and Barnett's "Chapel in the Field". The festival chorus offered a selection from "Jephtha" and the presiding organist's composition "Rhineland". Horace Hill's overture "May Morning" was played by the Norwich Philharmonic band.

After the 3rd item in the programme, the mayor, deputy mayor, the Dean, Sir Peter Eade, F. Oddin Taylor, P. E. Hansell and G. B. Kennett, the town clerk; took their places on the platform for the presentation. The mayor in his opening speech, mentioned how Bunnett had given 26 recitals that season attracting a welcome increase in the number of "working class". He hoped more such persons would be seen in the future as, with an admittance of just 2d, these recitals were mainly directed towards the poorer members of society. After giving a brief summary of Bunnett's life, the mayor presented him with an illuminated address, a cheque for £280 and a album bound in red morocco, containing the names of all the subscribers, written and illustrated by Mr. Fred Thwaites, one of Mr. Oddin Taylor's staff.

The illuminated address, mounted in a frame of gold and polished oak by Mr. Dimmock, had been on display in Dimmock's shop window at 66 London Street. Mr. F. O. Taylor read the inscription to the audience:-

"Presented to Edward Bunnett, Esq; Mus. Doc. (Cantab.) Fellow of the Royal College of Organists, and member of the Royal Incorporated Society of Musicians, 22 years assistant organist at Norwich cathedral, 24 years organist of the Norfolk and Norwich Festival, 19 years organist of the church of St Peter Mancroft, Norwich, and 16 years organist of the Norwich Corporation, together with a cheque for £280, on his attaining his musical jubilee, as a mark of admiration of his talents, and in recognition of the eminent services rendered by him to the art of music. Signed on behalf of the subscribers, John Moore (mayor) and F. Oddin Taylor (hon secretary), Norwich, April 1896".

The words were surrounded by a beautiful border incorporating the names of famous composers, a manuscript book, a pen, a baton and the arms of Corpus Christi and Trinity colleges where Bunnett had studied. Contained in the commencing capital "P" was a miniature picture of the cathedral. Loud applause filled the hall as the recipient came forward to reply. It was a proud moment for him. He recalled how it brought back memories of his early days when the orchestra was erected at the west end. The music he heard then was still vivid in his memory. Although his hopes of being the cathedral organist had not been fulfilled, he held with pride the position of corporation organist. In this capacity he had given over 400 recitals: a total of some 4000 pieces. Turning to the orchestra, Bunnett thanked the Philharmonic Society and the festival chorus for assisting him on so many occasions; their kindness being much appreciated. A special thank you was given to Dr. Horace Hill, Mr. F. W. B. Noverre and Miss Blamy, the latter having travelled from London to gratuitously perform vocal items such as Dudley Puck's "hackneyed" song "When the Heart is Young".

During the summer months Horace worked hard bringing the chorus to the highest possible standard for the festival which was again to have the presence of Royalty. The first concert was on 6th October. The day was cold and wet. As evening approached the precipitation increased, but still St. Andrew's Hall was fairly full. After Costa's arrangement of the National Anthem, the 326 strong band and chorus performed "Jephtha" while the rain fell unceasingly on the roof of the hall. The concert was a complete success.

The next morning brought sunshine. From dawn the city streets were busy with people hastily erecting decorations to welcome the Royal visitors who were expected around noon. The inclement weather of the previous day preventing this task. However many displays were abandoned as spectators took up their positions along the scheduled route.

At 11.30am the general public were barred from the yard at Thorpe station and the growing crowds outside were kept under control by a detachment of G. E. R. police from Liverpool Street station. At 11.45am a special train from Cromer carrying the Princess Louise and Lady Battersea steamed into platform 4. The couple had journeyed from Overstrand. Alighting from the saloon carriage Her Royal Highness was escorted to a specially prepared waiting room. At 12.00 noon the 10.33am train from Wolferton arrived at platform 3 carrying the Prince of Wales and the Duke and Duchess of York. Joining Princess Louise at the front entrance, amid a cheering crowd, the Royal party made their way to the awaiting carriages. The procession, headed by a detachment of mounted police, drove slowly up Prince of Wales Rd. The Union Jack and the Red Ensign projected from Hills and Underwood's distillery near Foundry Bridge. At Post Office Plain a mass of people watched as the procession turned into Bank Plain and passed the front of Barclay's Bank where an array of bannerets were displayed on a backdrop of crimson cloth. Turning into London Street the premises of G. W. Dimmock and those of Mr Bowhill opposite, were profusely decorated with flags. Further along the street, pretty small flags decorated Fasola's café. At the far end, Messrs. Jarrold showed a fine display of flags whilst the buildings on Howlett's corner had their balconies studded with shields. Turning right into Exchange St. the procession passed the establishment of Daniel Bros. who exhibited a magnificent collection of plants and evergreens.

At St. Andrew's Hall the party was greeted by Messrs. F. O. Taylor, honorary secretary of the festival; H. C. Bolingbroke, chairman of the orchestra committee and C. R. Gilman, chairman of the committee of management. Making their way along a crimson carpeted corridor adorned with plants, electric lighting illuminating the way, they entered the reception room. The walls hung with Indian tapestries and mirrors; oriental carpets covered the floor on which elegant old oak furniture was placed.

As they entered the hall the audience rose, remaining in this position until the National Anthem had been sung. It was well beyond the scheduled starting time of 11.45am. when A. C. Mackenzie made his way to the conductor's desk, bowing to the distinguished visitors before signalling for his "Rose of Sharon" to commence. The beautiful voice of Andrew Black was heard for the first time, making an excellent impression. Black was a native of Glasgow in which city he had held the post of church organist before turning to a singing career.

At the conclusion of the second part the mayor, Mr. J. Moore and the mayoress entertained the Royal party to luncheon in the old crypt; the descending stairway being draped in crimson cloth. Electric lights illuminated the vaulted ceiling giving a unique appearance. A large circular oak table was laid with 12 settings and side tables nestled against a backdrop of tapestry curtains. Groups of flowers added colour to the scene. After luncheon the Royal party returned to the hall; the oratorio resumed and at its conclusion they departed for the County Club. The morning sunshine had gone but despite heavy rain crowds still gathered outside.

The Royal party returned for the evening concert. The programme commenced with "Peer Gynt" suite No 1, followed by Parry's ode "Blest Pair of Sirens". The composer received a warm reception as he took his place to conduct what was to be a most splendid performance.

But it was a violin concerto by Frederick Cliffe, composed specially for the festival which proved to be the novelty of the evening. Although being well known as an orchestral composer this was Cliffe's first attempt at solo work. The part was played by M. Tivadar Nachez. The performance left a favourable impression and deserved greater applause but the conclusion coincided with the Royal visitors arising from their seats and retiring to the anti room before their departure for the 9.05pm train to Cromer and the 9.40pm to Wolferton.

The remainder of the concert was occupied with Randegger's

dramatic cantata "Fridolin". The words by Erminia Rudersdorff being based on a ballad by Schiller.

A performance of "Elijah" was given Thursday morning with fine weather adding to the enjoyment. In the evening Mancinelli conducted his new operatic cantata "Hero and Leander". The work, written in the "modern" style, had been composed expressly for the festival. The librettist, Sig. Arrigo Boito, on this occasion using the anagramatical nom de plume, "Tobia Gorrio".

Gounod's "Redemption" was performed on Friday morning and in the evening Stanford's ballad for chorus and orchestra, "Phaudrig Crohoone" was heard for the first time. This work, inspired by J. Sheridan Le Fanu's humorous poem, had been composed expressly for the festival. The concert closed with the 3rd act from "Lohengrin" sung to English words by Natalia Macfarren; the audience expressing their emotions to the full as the festival was brought to a close.

At a subsequent meeting of the festival committee, the mayor proposed that Horace should be made an honorary member of the committee of management, in recognition of his valued services over the past 15 years. It was met with a resounding "Hear, Hear".

CHAPTER 47

The Queen's Diamond Jubilee

A motor car was seen on the streets of Norwich for the first time on Thursday 19th November 1896. The vehicle a "Victoria", was introduced by the proprietor of a menagerie who was visiting the city at the time. It was described as being light and elegant in appearance. The only machinery visible was a "chain gear connecting the wheels". The car, ran "smoothly and without noise", attracting much attention. Those who so desired were allowed the opportunity to take a trip in the vehicle.

Early in the new year the members of the festival chorus were invited to a Conversazione in Blackfriars' Hall. The occasion afforded the mayor, C. R. Gilman, the opportunity to present Horace with a handsome gold watch, a copy of the recently published history of the Norfolk and Norwich musical festivals and an illuminated list of the all the subscribers, in recognition of his services to music. The presentation came as a complete surprise to the chorus master who thank his friends for their totally unexpected gift, saying how deeply grateful he was for their kindness and willingness to assist at all times. Horace's musical activities had recently digressed. He had given a lecture on the life and works of G. A Macfarren, with whom he had enjoyed a personal acquaintance, to the students of the School of Music. The lecture was repeated at Holy Trinity church hall, South Heigham in March, with the profits going towards reducing the debt on the newly erected Pelham Memorial Hall.

At the second A. G. M. of the School of Music held in April 1897, in the school's office, the chairman of the directors, C. R. Gilman, announced that the school was not yet self sufficient. However it had not been established to become a money making venture but to provide a musical education and this it did most successful. Students now competed for various medals and scholarships. A gold medal donated by Mrs. J. W. Rose was awarded to piano student Miss Ethel White and a silver medal given by Horace Hill was earned by Miss Eva Morley. Mr. F. T. Moffin gained the new "Bates" scholarship for singing, providing him with one year's free tuition with Dr. Bates. A similar scholarship for piano, awarded by Kingston Rudd, went to Mable Harrington and Miss Dorothy Whiteley achieved a violin scholarship under Mr. Noverre.

Everywhere people were looking forward to the celebrations for Queen Victoria's Diamond Jubilee.

Tuesday 22nd of June was "Jubilee Day" and declared a public holiday. The day dawned dull and overcast with not the slightest breeze to blow the masses of flags and bunting hanging over the city. As the church clocks chimed 8 o' clock, the bells of St. Peter's rang forth 60 volleys and then burst into a joyous peal. The bells had been set the previous night to eliminate the preliminary jangling so all 12 would fire at once. At 8.30am the bells ceased and the distant booming of cannon fire could be heard from the direction of Britannia Barracks, the immense puffs of smoke being visible from the castle as a 21 gun salute was fired.

After breakfast the streets began to fill with sightseers and a breeze brought life to the city's miles of decorations.

By 9.15am the Carrow Works band in their smart blue and white uniforms had taken up their positions in the Market Place. Soon school children paraded into the square to sing as others had done 10 years before. This time the conductor was Mr. C. Hubbard of Nelson Street Boys' School.

When noon approached the Market Place turned into a military parade ground, a "feu de joie" being fired in Her Majesty's honour.

At 1 o'clock prominent members of the city and county joined the mayor for luncheon in the Guildhall; the catering having been entrusted to Mr. R. F. Ladell of Gentleman's Walk. Throughout the day a host of activities were held for the enjoyment of the general public. The gardens of Chapelfield and Castle Meadow thronged with people as various bands played. A captive hot air balloon, under the supervision of experience aeronaut, Mr. Beckett, made frequent ascents from the cattle market at the rear of the Agricultural Hall. On each trip 5 persons floated 3000 feet above the city. In the afternoon, at the recreation ground on Earlham Rd., cycle and running races took place and also a decorated cycle parade for ladies and girls. Generous prizes were awarded to the winners.

Lakenham cricket ground hosted a novelty cricket match. The players being dressed in costumes representing characters and nationalities of the Victorian era; a photograph capturing their costumes before the game commenced. Mr. W. H. Loades' XI was formed by ;-

W. H. Loades (Captain) dressed as a Jameson raider;

W. C. Walton: the Duke of Wellington;

H.A.Smith: W. E. Gladstone
Hugh Goodwyn: a mail guard;
F. B. Williams: His Honour Paddy O'Brien;
E. Gissing: Mr. Pickwick;
J. Goodwyn: a Zulu;
C. B. Hill: a hussar of the Light Brigade;
T. P. Braybrooks: an Indian prince;
A. Smith: Roentgen rays;
E. Richardson: a Diamond Jubilee masher.

The opposition, Mr. Cowles' XI were:-
A. Cowles (Captain) dressed as John Bull;
L. G. Page: Rt. Hon. Benjamin Disraeli;
W. Smith: a schoolboy of 1837;
G. H. Salter: Dr. W. G. Grace;
C. T. Kerrison: a sailor of 1837;
A. Livock: an Australian gold digger;
Mr. Rivett: an agricultural labourer;
E.G. Collins: a swell of 1837;
T. B. Rix: an early volunteer;
J.W. Harper: a Victorian policeman;
W. Walton: The Mc.Pherson.

The umpires Mr. S. H. Smith and Robert Mason appeared as a British lion and Britannia. The costumes had been supplied by H. Nathan of 17 Coventry St., London and the important work of making up undertaken by Mr. Austen of London St, Norwich. Mr Cowles' team made 104 runs. Mr. Loades' team scored 107.

After the match the players paraded around the ground headed by the band of the V. B. N. R. Many spectators kept their handsome programme as a souvenir of the splendid afternoon of entertainment.

As darkness fell numerous illuminations decorated the city's buildings. On St. James' Hill an enormous bonfire was ignited by the deputy mayor. Within minutes of applying the torch, a pillar of flames 50 feet high rose into the night sky. It was one of many lit around the country at a specified time.

This whole day of festivities had passed off in an orderly manner without any arrests for drunkenness or bad conduct.

The inmates of the workhouse also celebrated the day. A special dinner was given in the workhouse dining hall which had been decorated with evergreens. A meal of beef, mutton, veal and ham was followed by plum pudding and fruit tarts, washed down with plenty of lemonade. The House Committee had decided that alcoholic beverages would be unwise. Each man received a supply of tobacco; each woman, sugar and tea and each child, a packet of sweets and an orange. Those persons who chose were allowed into the city in the afternoon, whilst the remaining inmates were given "high tea". In the evening the workhouse children toured the city in a cart to see the illuminations.

A handkerchief, bearing a portrait of the Queen, was given to every adult inmate by the mayor and sheriff to commemorate the occasion.

The aged poor were also not forgotten in this jubilation. On Thursday 24th June they were invited to a banquet in St. Andrew's Hall at 1.30pm. The weather was hot, preventing many from attending. Mr. Grix of the Central Café, Orford Place served a dinner of roast beef, roast leg and haunches of mutton, roast rib of beef and boiled leg of mutton, served with new potatoes, asparagus, peas and cabbage. Plum pudding, rhubarb and gooseberry tarts completed the meal which was helped on its way by a supply of ale and mineral water. The oldest guest was Mrs. Mary Ann Rix aged 91, of North Heigham.

That evening the mayor invited over 1300 guests to a reception in the castle; Dr. Horace Hill and Mrs. Hill being among them. As 8 o'clock approached the guests arrived, alighting from their carriages at the lodge gate. They passed through a covered passageway constructed over the bridge to the main entrance; the awning having been erected by D. Hurn of Dove St. The entrance lobby was decorated with a superb collection of exotic and flowering plants. The stone balustrade of the staircase leading to the keep was tastefully adorned with red, white and blue flowers entwined in smilax wreathing. On the south side of the corridor to the right of the entrance lobby, the mayor and mayoress received their guests. Opposite to them the massive silver gilt mace and civic sword was displayed on a table. Proceeding through the various departments of the museum the guests entered the keep by an entrance draped in heavy tapestries. The decoration of this ancient pile had been entrusted to Messrs. Holborn and Co. of Wensum Street. Oriental rugs, bordered by a margin of crimson cloth covered the floor upon which rested luxurious lounges and ottomans. The walls remained free from any additional embellishments to show off their natural beauty.

In the north gallery the Carrow band led by Mr. Jackson played a selection of popular tunes including "The Diamond Jubilee" by Kappey and a barn dance "Boston Belle" by C. Godfrey, their programme ending with "God Save the Queen". During the course of the evening many guests paraded the picture gallery. Their promenade being accompanied by Howlett's orchestra playing marches such as "Her Majesty's Record Reign" by F. Rose.

A massive refreshment pavilion measuring 62 feet by 40 feet, erected in the courtyard, could accommodate 500 guests at any one time. Its crimson interior walls, panelled in 3 shades of yellow, were adorned with trophies and shields. Crimson cloth covered the floor. The task of catering for this large gathering had been committed to the capable hands of Mr. Snelling.

Another temporary pavilion, placed in the most convenient of positions in the courtyard, acted as a ladies and gentlemen's cloakroom. At 11 o'clock the company departed.

After this week of festivities the city returned to its normal routine. The Norfolk and Norwich School of Music ended their summer term on 30th July with a musical evening. For the first time the mandolin and organ featured in the programme. In the absence of the mayor, the lady mayoress presented the medals and scholarships contested during the term.

Additional medals from leading Norwich citizens were promised for the future.

The school concluded 1897 with a harp recital by Aptommas, playing a Lyon and Healy instrument. Although just 5 days before Christmas, this Thursday afternoon recital attracted a large audience. As they entered, each person was handed a printed paper listing a number of well known melodies. One piece was to be nominated, that receiving the most votes being added to the recital's programme. The "Moonlight" sonata and the "Turkish Patrol" gained near equal popularity, both received a performance amidst arrangements by Aptommas of Welsh melodies, English folk tunes and American airs plus an Etude and Tarenelle of his own composition.

CHAPTER 48

The Death of J.J. Colman

The first of the festival chorus's interim concerts took place in December 1897 when a performance of "Faust" was given. During the following 3 months Spohr's "Last Judgement" and Rossini's "Stabat Mater" were perpared for their second concert on the 24th March 1898. At the last moment one of the 4 soloists, Mr. William Green, fell ill and his place was taken by Mr. J. Leyland. This sudden change did not detract from the quality of the performance as the perfect singing of the quartet "Quando Corpus" in the "Stabat Mater" triggered an eruption of enthusiastic applause from the audience. Throughout the concert the chorus master kept his forces well in hand: every beat was carefully observed. His painstaking labours accumulating into two highly gratifying performances.

Shortly afterwards Horace became involved with the musical arrangements for the Missionary Loan Exhibition which commenced in the Agricultural Hall on 18th April. This week long event celebrated the jubilee of the Church Missionary Society (13). The purpose of the exhibition was to attract an interest in the society's work of bringing Christianity to the heathen in various parts of the world. On the closing Saturday Horace conducted a choir of boys from the Model School. In the evening he was torn between 2 events. Having commenced the conducting of Dr. Bunnett's end of series concert, Horace handed the baton to Bunnett after the performance of Handel's organ concerto in F major and returned to the Agricultural Hall for the closing ceremony. Canon Pelham Burn summed up the weeks activities and announced the exhibition had attracted 35,000 visitors raising £1560, every penny of which would go towards the Mission's cause, once expenses had been paid..

On 18th May 1898 the Norwich Philharmonic gave their 95th concert. Horace had the pleasurable task of conducting Bruch's violin concerto No 1. The soloist was Mary Noverre. The lady had recently achieved her A.R.C.M. with great credit. Her brilliant execution of the concerto brought rounds of applause from the packed Noverre room, Mary having to return to bow her acknowledgement before their appreciative demonstration subsided.

As Whitsuntide approached news reached the city of the

Automobile Club's pending visit. Having motored from London to Cambridge on Friday 27th May, the club arrived on Saturday 28th May by way of Newmarket, Bury St Edmunds, Thetford, Attleborough and Wymondham. That evening they dined at the newly opened Royal Hotel at Bank Plain. The vehicles left Norwich on Whit Monday for Ipswich. The dawn skies were bright and with the Castle Museum being the only other holiday attraction in the city, few stayed to witness their departure.

Thorpe station thronged with people making their way to the coast. 7600 took trains to Yarmouth, 1700 to Lowestoft and 600 to Cromer. 400 travelled to Brundall and 300 to Wroxham. Others journeyed further afield to Cambridge and 100 ventured as far as Edwinstowe to visit the Dukeries.

The City station also bustled with people as another 700 people made their way to Cromer. The regattas at Coldham Hall and Cantley also proved to be popular attractions. Nearer to home wagonettes rolled into Thorpe Village and the villages of Mulbarton and Cossey were a favourite destination for cyclists.

In July it was the turn of the juvenile and aged poor of the workhouse to enjoy a day out. On a Friday morning 200 eligible inmates were loaded into 21 wagonettes. The procession, headed by a brass band under the direction of Mr. J.W. Eastick, drew much attention as it passed through the streets to Foundry Bridge. Here the supervised party of 122 old men, 37 old women and 38 children, boarded the steamer "Jenny Lind". The youngest member of the party was just 5 years of age; the eldest man was 90; the eldest women, 92. Those in control had forbidden the oldest inmate Mrs. Elizabeth Tiptod to go. The woman had been at the workhouse for 17 years and was thought to be too infirm. She was deeply offended and expressed her displeasure most forcefully, threatening to leave the institution and walk to London.

The "Jenny Lind" cruised down to Cantley. Refreshments were served en route. On their return they stopped at Whitlingham where a substantial dinner was provided by Mr. C. Betts, the proprietor of the Criterion restaurant in White Lion Street. Games, races and other entertainment occupied the time until the steamer departed at 7 o'clock. On its arrival at Foundry Bridge 1 hour later, the wagonettes awaited to ferry the inmates back to the workhouse. Throughout the day young and old continually thanked the organisers for the trip which had been provided by public subscription.

On 18th September 1898 Norwich lost one of its most benevolent and respected citizens, Mr. J.J. Colman. His death was mourned throughout the city. On the morning of the funeral the bells of St. Peter Mancroft rang forth a muffled peal and shades were drawn across the windows of many buildings. Outside Thorpe station crowds gathered to await the arrival of a special train from Corton bearing the coffin from the family's seaside retreat.

At 2 o'clock the train pulled into platform 6. Relatives and friends watched as the many floral tributes were removed before the coffin was reverently lifted from the carriage onto the hearse. By a quarter past two all the invited mourners had taken their places in the Prince's Street chapel and spent the next quarter of an hour in "quietude" as Dr. Bunnett softly played the organ. After the service, conducted by the Rev. Barrett, the funeral procession made its way to the Rosary cemetery through streets lined with citizens wishing to pay their last respects. Around the roped off family grave many more had gathered. Among them stood representatives from the Norfolk and Norwich Musical Festival and the School of Music. Hundreds of Carrow workers, both male and female, occupied the knoll. As they waited for the funeral cortège the Carrow band solemnly played. Such a sight had never before been witnessed and for those present, never to be forgotten. After the committal, the sound of Mendelssohn's "Funeral March" could be heard as mourners filed past the graveside. The day closed with the bells of St. Peter Mancroft ringing out another muffled peal.

CHAPTER 49

Elgar's "Sea Pictures"

The city streets had begun to take on a new appearance. Gangs of workmen were gauging their way through St. Giles Street and Prince of Wales Rd. to lay tram lines.

The festival chorus revived Beethoven's "Ruins of Athens" for their last interim concert before the 1899 festival. The work had recently been set to English words giving it a new lease of life.

The Norfolk and Norwich School of Music now enjoyed prosperity with over 100 students. Horace had lectured on "Scottish Songs" in the autumn term of 1898. In the new year of 1899 piano student Mabel Harrington gained her L.R.A.M.

Mrs. Tiptod, the workhouse inmate, reached her 100th birthday on January 18th. Although 6 months earlier she was declared too infirm to participate in the boat trip, the woman was now said to be in good health, retained all her faculties; read without the aid of spectacles and enjoyed a bath each morning.

Dohnányi

In February the pianist, Herr von Dohnányi, was introduced to the city. His playing was described as "ferocious" at times; nothing but the most powerfully built piano being able to withstand his muscular treatment.

His visit was shortly followed by the return of Paderewski who gave another recital on 16th March organised by Messrs. Howlett and Son. Another Good Friday performance of the "Messiah" was given under the direction of Dr. Hill and Dr. Bunnett, but the Easter plans to open the city's new Royal Arcade had to be deferred until May.

Horace had been composing a new overture. Its first performance was given at the Norwich Philharmonic's 97th concert on 24th May 1899. The work entitled "Dussin's Dale" showed off his contrapuntal skills and concluded with an animated coda. Loud applause followed bringing this gifted musician back to the platform to bow his acknowledgement.

Clara Butt

Since the beginning of the year Horace had been training the chorus for the next festival. During the month of September at least 3 evenings each week were devoted to rehearsals. It was publicly declared that Horace was the "main stay" of the festival "without the painstaking work done by him and his assistants the festival would be impossible".

The festival's first concert on the evening of Tuesday 3rd October was entirely devoted to Berlioz "Faust". The hall portrayed a most brilliant appearance. At the east end, the bright red temporary gallery formed the backdrop for the chorus. The ladies dresses, adorned with pink or blue sashes, contrasted with the darker attire of the gentlemen. The whole scene gleamed in the electric lighting. The next morning Clara Butt made her debut before a Norwich audience, singing Dvorak's "Biblical Songs" accompanied on the organ by Dr. Bunnett and on the piano by Kingston Rudd. Her expressive rendering brought forth hearty applause, recalling her to the platform to bow in acknowledgement. This morning's programme also included Verdi's "Stabat Mater", "Laudi alla Vergine Maria" and "Te Deum". The works being heard for the first time in Norwich. The "Laudi alla Vergine Maria", scored for vocal quartet, was sung on this occasion by Ethel Wood, Kelyn Williams, Julia Franks and Ethel Nutter, the ladies wearing white gowns with red sashes. New music also featured in the evening concert where Saint Saëns' opera "Samson and Delila" was brought before a Norwich audience for the first time.

On Thursday the hall was occupied by a rather small audience of 1,073. Many vacant seats were visible. Young Mr. Edward Elgar commenced the concert by conducting the first performance in the city of his Mediation "Lux Christi". He was seen to handle the performers with "the skill of an artist". The work was well received causing Elgar to twice return to the platform in response to the audience's demands. After Gounod's recitative and air "Lend Me Your Aid" from "Reine de Saba" sung by Edward Lloyd, Don Lorenzo Perosi's sacred trilogy "The Passion of Christ", heard for the first time in England, concluded Part I.

Parry received a cordial welcome as he took his place at the conductor's desk to commence the second part with his ode "A Song of Darkness and Light". This too had never been performed before a Norwich audience and was met with appreciative applause.

Edward Elgar

In the evening Elgar returned to the concert platform to conduct the first performance of his new song cycle "Sea Pictures" which he had written expressly for the festival. The soloist was Clara Butt. At its conclusion the work received an enthusiastic response. Elgar was reluctant to come forward and had to be coaxed on to the platform by Clara. Four times they bowed to the audience, then Clara turned towards him and graciously bowed in homage.

The first part of the programme concluded with Edward German's symphonic suite "The Seasons" this work too was composed expressly for the festival. After Frederic Cowen's setting of "Ode to the Passions" and his "Dream of Endymion" both of which were new to Norwich, this lengthy musical evening concluded at 11.30pm with the overture "Di Ballo" by Sullivan. With the exception of those who had to catch their trains home few had left the hall early.

Friday morning found a return of Handel's "Messiah" and in the evening Coleridge Taylor's "Hiawatha's Wedding Feast" was followed by an all Wagner second part. Edward Lloyd made his farewell appearance being cheered as he completed a performance of "Prize Lied" from "Die Meistersingers".

The 1899 festival closed with the march and chorus from "Tannhäuser", having made a profit of £400.

A few days later it was announced that Horace had been elected a Member of the London College of Music, to fill the vacancy caused by the death of Dr. Walter Sangster. The Norfolk and Norwich School of Music was still the local examination centre of the College. Trinity College also used the school for examinations and on a Friday afternoon in early November 1899 Dr. E. H. Turpin, lecturer, organist and warden of the college was invited to distribute the certificates. In his address Turpin spoke of his pleasure in coming to Norwich, a city with a great musical tradition of which he had been aware since childhood. He was sure this memorable visit to the city would remain with him for the rest of his life. Before handing out certificates to 61 successful candidates Turpin imparted valued advice on the importance of examinations.

As Christmas approached people's thoughts turned to those fighting in the Boer War. A consignment of Christmas puddings made by the womenfolk of the city had been dispatched to the front and citizens made the best of the festive holiday. The pleasant sunny weather on Christmas Day brought many people out into

Coleridge Taylor

the streets but cyclists were few owing to the muddy conditions of the roads. On Boxing Day rain fell continuously. Many attended the fair and an afternoon football match between C.E.Y.M.S and Kirkley on the Earlham Rd. recreation ground also proved a big attraction. A musical comedy "The Belle of New York" was being staged at the theatre and Gilbert's circus was at the Agricultural Hall. On 27th December reservist of the Norfolk regiment assembled at Britannia Barracks. The next morning 320 soldiers marched down St. James' Hill, Bishopgate, Palace Street, Tombland, King Street and Prince of Wales Rd. to Thorpe station. 1000's gathered to watch, many marching alongside them. Women wept as they said "Good Bye" to their loved ones. At a quarter to eleven a train 7 carriages long, carried their loved ones out of the station as bands played "Auld Lang Syne". Soldiers hung out of every window waving. On the station friends and relatives cheered and cried until the train was out of sight.

Edmund Turpin

CHAPTER 50

Death of Horace Hill

By February 1900 the womenfolk of the city had received the unwelcome news that their consignment of Christmas puddings to the front line had deteriorated over the long journey arriving totally inedible. Their greetings cards too had become indecipherable with the exception of one from Mrs. Vaughan Thomas. This lady received a letter of thanks explaining the disappointment felt by the men. Although their efforts had been in vain the men drew comfort from the knowledge that unknown friends showed concern over their welfare. Back home, Norfolk was in the grip of a foot and mouth outbreak and had little idea of the hardships the men were enduring.

The Norwich Philharmonic gave their 98th concert on 15th February. Horace took up his usual place at the conductor's desk, having spent the day teaching at Great Yarmouth. The weather had been foul and the dreadful conditions consequently effected the concert's attendance. The Noverre Room was barely half full but Horace still carried out his duties with the utmost care as the band played Kalliwoda's Symphony No 1 in F minor, and Spohr's Symphony No 2 in D minor. The programme also featured 2 movements of Beethoven's trio in B♭ and 2 movements from Weber's quintet for clarionet and strings. Further variety was added to the programme with vocal contributions by Miss Adela Tunbridge of Great Yarmouth, and Miss Lansdell aged 16, a resident of the city, whose rich mellow contralto voice astonished her audience. Their singing was accompanied on the piano by Frank Hill. Unfortunately a harp solo by Mr. W. J. Blake had to be omitted; the bad state of the roads prevented him from being present.

Six days later Horace travelled to North Walsham by omnibus to conduct the musical society's concert in the church rooms. The principal works were Rossini's "Stabat Mater" and Mendelssohn's "42nd Psalm" with the addition of miscellaneous solo items sung by Miss Nutter, Miss Rix, Mr. Murray Ramsey and Mr. E. Freeman. These included some patriotic songs which excited the audience, particularly one entitled "The War" by Claud Hill sung by Miss Rix who on demand, repeated the last verse.

Horace journeyed home the same night with several friends. He unwisely chose to take the box seat. A few days afterwards he developed a severe cold confining him to his house for 2 weeks. Although weak his spirit for work would not leave him and he resumed his teaching duties on Tuesday 13th March.

On the Thursday he went to Great Yarmouth to give lessons, returning to Thorpe Station at 5.50pm. One of his daughters was there to meet him. They walked out of the station together and caught a wagonette bound for the city. On crossing Foundry Bridge Horace became faint. Fellow passenger Mr. Barwell of London Street, summoned the driver, Mr. Daniels, to stop. Brandy was procured and attempts were made to find a doctor in the area. All were out, except Dr. Williams who himself was too ill to leave his residence. Horace was carried to the surgery but it was too late, this much loved, respected, talented musician had died.

CODA

That evening members of the Philharmonic gathered for a meeting unaware of the tragedy. As they awaited the arrival of Dr. Hill the melancholy news of his death at the age of 67 was brought to them.

His funeral took place the following Monday. An open hearse bearing the coffin smothered in floral tributes and 3 mourning coaches left Horace's St Stephen's home at 11.30am.

At the Earlham cemetery gates the family mourners were joined by a procession headed by Canon Owen representing North Walsham Musical Society and the Rev. H. W. Wimble of Paston Grammar school. They were followed by Dr. Bates, Dr. Bunnett and Mr. W. Heaver representing the Norfolk and Norwich School of Music; members of the festival chorus and of the Philharmonic Society. Many pupils and friends of the deceased were also present. The service was conducted by the Rev. J. Callis of Holy Trinity, Heigham and the Rev. T. Stone, vicar of St. James' church in the city where Horace had worshipped for the past 2 years and his youngest son was organist.

The service in the cemetery chapel and at the graveside was kept simple. To comply with the wishes of the grieving family, Horace Hill was interred without a single note of music.

In the evening the festival chorus met at the School of Music and at their request the bells of St. Peter Mancroft rang forth a muffled peal as a tribute to his memory. After 418 changes the tenor bell tolled the age of the deceased across the city.

1= *PRO 1841 census, reference 788/10, enumerator schedule15, page 12*
2= *NRO SO33/6*
3= *White's directory of Norfolk 1845*
4= *St. Gregory's Parish Marriage Records. Page 58, No. 116.*
5= *Hunt's directory of Norwich 1850*
6= *PRO 1851 census index reference 1816/48/12*
7= *NRO SO33/7*
8= *Wymondham Abbey Marriage Records. Page 42, Document No.88.*
9= *NRO MS 33223 725x7*
10= *"Degrees in Music" by Abdy Williams. Published 1893.*
11= *PRO 1871 census reference 225, RG10/1816 ecclesiastical district 118, page 7.*
12= *NRO PD 192/62*
13= *Norfolk Annals.*
14= *NRO WD19 384x*
15= *PRO 1881 census CD rom. F.H.L. film 1341471. reference RG11, Piece1956, Folio 19, page 7 and F.H.L.film 1341469 RG11 Piece 1947, Folio 26, page 8.*
16= *NRO SO33/10*
17= *NRO SO33/11*
18= *PRO 1891 census reference 225, RG12, 1527, Fiche no. 1 page 2 schedule 10.*
19= *Hamilton's directory of Norwich 1879*
All other information from the newspapers the "Norwich Mercury", the "Norfolk Chronicle" and the "Annals of the Norfolk and Norwich Triennial Musical Festivals" by R. H. Legge and W. E. Hansell published by Jarrold in 1896.

Acknowledgements.
I would like to acknowledge my sincere thanks to:-
The Local Studies Library and the Norfolk Record Office for their valued assistance throughout my research.
The E.D.P. for the use of information and quotes from the "Norwich Mercury" and "Norfolk Chronicle".
The Public Record Office, "New Grove Dictionaries", "The Musical Times", Norwich City Council, Dereham Town Council, Jarrold and Sons Ltd. and Kelly's Directories.